The Journey of Christian Initiation

The Journey of Christian Initiation

Theological and pastoral perspectives

John Hind
Paul Avis (Editor)
Martin Davie
Harriet Harris
Christopher Hill
Stephen Platten

The Faith and Order Commission
of the General Synod of the Church of England

CHURCH HOUSE
PUBLISHING

Published 2011 for the
Faith and Order Commission
of the General Synod of
the Church of England.

Church House Publishing
Church House, Great Smith Street,
London, SW1P 3AZ

Email: copyright@churchofengland.org

British Library Cataloguing in Publication Data

A catalogue record for this book is available
from the British Library

978 0 7151 4237 0

Typeset in 9.5pt Stone Sans
by RefineCatch Limited, Bungay, Suffolk
Printed and bound in Great Britain by
CPI Antony Rowe, Chippenham, Wiltshire

Contents

Contributors

John Hind is Bishop of Chichester, Chairman of the Faith and Order Commission of the Church of England and a Vice-President of the World Council of Churches' Faith and Order Commission.

Paul Avis is General Secretary of the Council for Christian Unity, Canon Theologian of Exeter and honorary professor at the University of Exeter.

Martin Davie is the Theological Consultant of the House of Bishops and Theological Secretary of the Council for Christian Unity.

Harriet Harris is Chaplain of the University of Edinburgh.

Christopher Hill is the Bishop of Guildford, Chairman of the Council for Christian Unity and a Vice-President of the Conference of European Churches.

Stephen Platten is the Bishop of Wakefield and Chairman of the Church of England's Liturgical Commission.

Foreword

This project is the swansong of FOAG – the Faith and Order Advisory Group – which has served the theological and ecumenical agenda of the Church of England for 40 years. The Group, now merged with the House of Bishops' Theological Group and the Doctrine Commission into the newly constituted Faith and Order Commission of the Church of England (FAOC) has always been at its best when considering the ecumenical implications of theological questions or the theological implications of ecumenical questions. Few topics better illustrate this approach than the sacraments of Christian initiation. (I hope that even those who do not much like the term, will tolerate it as a convenient shorthand!)

The title of the first essay in this collection 'Pilgrimage of Grace' assumes an answer to at least one question of controversy: 'Is initiation a moment or a process?' As a pilgrimage, a journey, a process, it is, however, marked by particular moments. The relation of these moments to each other, the weight to be given to each of them and their order has sometimes been a cause of dispute between Christians even within the same ecclesial family. Among Anglicans, it is enough to mention the long battles over baptismal regeneration and the nature of confirmation, or the current debate over 'baptismal ecclesiology' or the 'baptismal covenant'. To my mind it is dangerous to play 'baptismal' and 'eucharistic' ecclesiologies off against each other, and to do so can easily lead to merely functional views of ordained ministry or to the reduction of ordination to a kind of commissioning for service.

'Pilgrimage of Grace' also reminds us of one of the most bitter periods of religious controversy in England, in the sixteenth century, and so too of the need for the disciples of Jesus to be and be seen to be 'of one heart and mind'.

These essays are intended both to help members of the Church of England to think through some of the theological and ecumenical dimensions of Christian initiation and offered to the wider Church as a contribution to our growing up into Christ – together.

FOAG has sometimes produced common reports, and at other times has, as in the present collection of essays, worked together on papers prepared by individual members of the Group who have generously submitted their drafts for the scrutiny and advice of the Group as a whole. I am grateful for the efforts of those who have contributed to this particular project and also take this opportunity to pay tribute to all the members and staff who have served FOAG with their knowledge, wisdom and insight over the years.

John Hind, Bishop of Chichester
Chairman of FOAG and FAOC
July 2010

1

Introduction: Christian initiation – a pilgrimage of grace

Paul Avis

We cannot get very far in the Church's work of pastoral care, evangelization or ecumenism without coming up against challenging issues concerning Christian initiation. There are some very practical questions hovering around this area of ministry. Indeed, it seems that there is considerable uncertainty, not to say confusion among Anglicans on matters of Christian initiation – though this uncertainty is not unique to Anglicans. Some of the practical issues, related to Christian initiation, that arise in the contexts of pastoral care, evangelization and ecumenism are:

- Should a new Christian, who has been baptized in infancy, be baptized again on profession of faith?

- Do the churches recognize each other's baptisms, so that those moving from one church to another do not need to be re-baptized?

- Why does the Church confirm those who have been baptized, even as adults, and what difference does confirmation make?

- Does it make sense to describe baptism as 'full sacramental initiation'?

- Why does the Church of England insist that baptized persons should be confirmed, or 'ready and desirous to be confirmed' in order to receive Holy Communion?

- Can the Church of England accept, for its own purposes, confirmation by a presbyter in non-episcopal partner churches?

The term 'Christian initiation' refers to the beginning of the Christian life, to the way in which new Christians are led to participate fully, through the sacraments, in the life of grace within the Church. Christian initiation encompasses what the Christian Church believes and practises about preparation for baptism (catechesis), baptism itself, personal profession of faith, confirmation and first communion.

Although 'initiation' is not a biblical word – neither is Trinity, for that matter – it is a useful portmanteau term for the journey of faith, and the major milestones on that journey, that leads us to share fully in the sacramental life of the Church. Christian initiation is a journey into grace.

This report is intended to clarify and reaffirm the Church of England's understanding of Christian initiation. We ground our discussion in the New Testament and the early Church and set what we have to say in the context of the development of the Church's theology and practice of initiation from the mediaeval and Reformation periods up to the present. We draw on the Book of Common Prayer (1662), the Thirty-nine Articles and *Common Worship*, as well as on Scripture and the Church's tradition.

Our studies show that, although there has always been some variety in how initiation has been understood, a clear basic pattern eventually emerged in the Western Church before the Reformation – a pattern that has been continued in the Church of England, in the Roman Catholic Church and in a number of Protestant churches to the present day. Our aim is to bring that pattern and process into focus and to consider some of the theological and practical issues that it raises for us today.

The pattern that we discern in the New Testament and the Church's tradition sees the sacrament of baptism as standing at the heart of Christian initiation, but not as the whole of it. Baptism unites us to Christ in his death and resurrection (Rom. 6.3ff; Gal. 3.27). Baptism is the work of the Holy Spirit; it is the sacrament of new birth within the fellowship of the Church, which is the Body of Christ (John 3.5; 1 Cor. 12.13; Eph. 5.26–27).

We are baptized in the Name of the Father and of the Son and of the Holy Spirit, one God in Trinity, and so brought into a new relationship with the Triune God in the Church of God (Matt. 28.19). This act of incorporation into the Body of Christ through the action of the Holy Spirit is clearly something so momentous and final that it cannot be repeated – though it can be claimed by faith and lived into more and more as life goes on. As the Scriptures and the Creed both affirm, there is only 'one baptism' (Eph. 4.5). Baptism is one of the greatest gifts that God gives us.

Baptism needs proper preparation – to use the language of the early Church, 'catechesis' – and it needs to be followed up with continued teaching within the Church. Baptism is followed by confirmation when we are strengthened by the Holy Spirit through the laying on of hands (in the Church of England this is always done by a bishop) in order that we may grow in grace day by day and exercise the manifold gifts of the Holy Spirit that Christ, the anointed one (Messiah), himself received and demonstrated. Emerging from the waters of the River Jordan, Jesus himself – though he came into the world through the action of the Holy Spirit and grew in grace through the presence of the Spirit in him (Luke 1.35, 2.52) – received a further empowering of the Spirit for his mission (Mark 1.10; Matt. 3.16; Luke 3. 21–22; John 1.32).

The members of the apostolic community, similarly – though many of them would have undergone the baptism of John the Baptist – received the outpouring of the Spirit at Pentecost (Acts 2.1–4), as well as subsequently (Acts 4.31). However, Saul of Tarsus was filled with the Spirit through the laying on of Ananias' hands prior to being baptized (Acts 9.17–18). In a similar way, the Spirit fell on the household of Cornelius as they received the gospel message, and that event pointed to the need for them to be baptized (Acts 10. 44–48).

The Holy Spirit acts in a sovereign way, but in the Church and especially where spiritual gifts are concerned, 'all things should be done decently and in order' (1 Cor. 14.40). 'Church Order' seeks to follow the Scriptures and the early Church in expressing a normative sequence of events, the norm. However, The Acts of the Apostles implies that there can be some flexibility in the order of events in Christian initiation. Admission of children to Holy Communion before confirmation might be an example of this flexible response to the work of the Spirit.

As the Book of Common Prayer (1662) rite of confirmation claims, the administration of confirmation after baptism follows the example of the Apostles when, according to The Acts of the Apostles, they laid hands on new converts that they might receive the Holy Spirit, even though the Spirit was already clearly at work in their lives, leading them to repentance and faith (Acts 8.14–17; 19.1–7). The incidents in The Acts are not a definitive model for confirmation – the circumstances of the apostolic church were in some respects unique – but as the Prayer Book says, they are an example. The Apostles did not act in a random manner. Their actions were not arbitrary. A basic pattern is apparent and the pattern is that baptism does not stand alone in terms of Christian initiation.

Confirmation provides an opportunity for those baptized in infancy to profess the faith of the Church for themselves (though it is important to say straight away that this is not the main purpose of confirmation). But confirmation is equally relevant to those who have been baptized at a time when they were able to profess the faith for themselves, for it is primarily God who confirms (that is to say, strengthens). God is the acting subject in the act of confirmation. The present report affirms the integrity of confirmation as an outward visible sign of an inward spiritual grace and its vital place in the overall process of Christian initiation.

United with Christ in baptism, strengthened and gifted by the Spirit in confirmation, we are sustained in our ongoing Christian life and witness by sharing in the celebration of the Church's Eucharist and by receiving Holy Communion. First communion is the culmination of Christian initiation: at that point we are led to participate fully in the life of grace that God has provided in the Church. We are brought into communion (*koinonia*) with the body and blood of Christ and with the Church as his body (1 Cor. 11.16–17). Although we still fall far short of what we should be as Christians, we are then ready to serve the Lord, our fellow Christians and our neighbour in discipleship and to respond to a call to some form of ministry when it comes.

As the *Common Worship* initiation services bring out so clearly, all this is a journey, a process, in which we make our pilgrimage closer to the heart of God and to the fellowship of Christ's Church. Baptism stands at the heart of Christian initiation, but it is not all there is to initiation. Confirmation is an important further step, a subsequent gift, and initiation is not complete until we have made our first communion. This is the sequence and pattern that has been followed in the Western Church for many centuries, long prior to the Reformation, and which continues to be taught and practised by the Church of England and by most other Anglican Churches, by the Roman Catholic Church and by major Protestant Churches. (The Eastern Churches practise a unified rite of initiation, mainly of infants, which includes several moments, including exorcism, baptism, chrismation and communion.)

Most Christian churches recognize one another's baptisms when they are performed with water, by immersion or pouring, in the name of the Holy Trinity, and with the intention 'to do what the Church does'. Baptist and Pentecostal churches are not able to subscribe to this ecumenical consensus because, unlike the vast majority of churches, they do not accept the baptism of infants or children. The report of the conversations between the Council for Christian Unity and the Baptist Union of Great Britain *Pushing at the Boundaries of Unity* (2005) suggested that there was a common pattern of initiation between our two traditions and that, when baptism was seen within that wider context, Baptists might be able to recognize the Anglican baptism of those not old enough to answer for themselves as true baptism. There is further discussion of this proposal in the essays that follow.

Mutual recognition of confirmation between the churches is less straightforward than mutual recognition of baptism. The Church of England accepts the episcopal confirmation (or chrismation in the case of the Orthodox Churches) of churches that are ordered in the historic episcopate, even though very often this is administered by the parish priest, using holy oil consecrated by the bishop. But not all churches with whom we share the historic episcopate practise episcopal confirmation. In the Nordic and Baltic Lutheran Churches, with whom the British and Irish Anglican Churches are in communion through the Porvoo Agreement of 1996, presbyteral confirmation is the norm. In the United Churches of South Asia, who are members of the Anglican Communion, provision is sometimes made for confirmation to be administered by presbyters (in both cases generally without the use of unction previously consecrated by the bishop). The Church of England accepts the baptisms, eucharistic celebrations and holy orders of these churches, with whom it is in communion, as interchangeable with its own: does it accept their confirmations? At the present time that is not clear and these essays are intended to help the Church to answer that question.

Then there are other churches, with whom we have important agreements of mutual recognition and mutual commitment – especially the Evangelische Kirche in Deutschland (EKD) and the Methodist Church of Great Britain – where a form of confirmation similar to our own is administered by the local presbyter. Under the present rules of the Church of England, those so confirmed must be episcopally confirmed if they wish to proceed to ordination or Readership in the Church of England. Both the EKD and the Methodist Church find this restriction very difficult to accept and both churches have recently formally requested that the Church of England consider whether this requirement could be relaxed in the light of the Meissen Agreement and the Anglican–Methodist Covenant respectively. The present report does not propose a particular answer to that request, but raises it for discussion within the councils of the Church.

2

Is baptism 'complete sacramental initiation'?[1]

Paul Avis

A cathedral newsletter invites candidates to come forward for confirmation preparation classes, stating: 'the Church of England believes that baptism is complete sacramental initiation'. Naturally, if they had already received complete sacramental initiation in baptism, nothing very positive could then be said about why anyone should want to be confirmed! However, I do not think that the Church of England officially believes that baptism is complete sacramental initiation and never has done. In this paper I want to challenge a modern misconception that enjoys wide currency in the churches, including the Church of England and other Churches of the Anglican Communion. It has come to be widely assumed that baptism comprises the whole of sacramental initiation. This view, which I will designate as 'BACSI' – 'Baptism As Complete Sacramental Initiation' – seems to have achieved the status of unquestioned orthodoxy.

I hope to make out a case for Christian initiation to be seen as a process that involves several essential elements, including, of course and crucially, baptism. But I oppose the commonly held view that baptism constitutes 'complete sacramental initiation', or even (as is sometimes said) 'complete initiation' as such (presumably including non-sacramental aspects, such as instruction in

---

1 A variant of this paper, under the same title, was published in *Theology* CXI, 861 (May–June 2008), pp. 163–9. A version was also given at the Fifth Theological Conference under the Meissen Agreement between the Church of England and the Evangelische Kirche in Deutschland (EKD) at Fox Hill, near Chester, in September 2005. That conference found remarkable agreement between the initiation liturgies of the two participating churches and theological convergence on Christian initiation as a process. For further discussion of the Anglican understanding of baptism see P. Avis, *The Identity of Anglicanism* (London and New York: T&T Clark, 2008), Chapter VI, 'Anglicanism and Baptismal Ecclesiology'.

the faith). I argue that confirmation is an act of a sacramental nature. Even though it is not a dominical sacrament – that is, one instituted by our Lord – on the same level as baptism and the Eucharist, confirmation has a fundamentally sacramental character as 'an outward and visible sign of an inward and spiritual grace, given unto us', as the Prayer Book Catechism, following an ancient Christian tradition, puts it. It would certainly be perverse to claim that confirmation is an unsacramental act! I further argue that confirmation has a vital place in Christian initiation, and that participating in the celebration of the Eucharist and receiving Holy Communion, normally for the first time, which are of course sacramental matters, are also an essential part of initiation and the culmination of the process.

Anglicans have struggled with the issues around Christian initiation for decades and many Anglicans, like other Christians, remain rather uncertain, if not confused, on this matter. Initiation is an ecumenical problem and there is probably no church that can be completely satisfied that its theology and practice leave no loose ends in this area. At this point I will mention (selectively) several milestones in modern Anglican reflection on initiation in order to show the context in which the idea of baptism as complete sacramental initiation (BACSI) first emerged.

Some key modern Anglican texts

(a) The report of the Commission on Christian Doctrine, that was set up by the Archbishops of Canterbury and York in 1922 and chaired by William Temple, *Doctrine in the Church of England*, affirmed the need for confirmation and laid down that it should precede admission to Holy Communion. Confirmation, according to the report, consists of prayer for the Holy Spirit (the form) and the laying on of hands of the bishop (the matter). The renewal of baptismal promises by the candidate, the report claimed, 'is not an essential element in the rite'. The Holy Spirit is given to strengthen the Christian and 'all theologians agree' on this. The Spirit brings the messianic gifts mentioned in Isaiah 11, so that, in confirmation, the candidate, 'already incorporated into Christ in baptism, is made a partaker in the gifts proper to the messianic community and its mission to the world'. The report is clear that 'there is a real gift of grace bestowed in Confirmation'. It argues that 'it is appropriate that the rite wherein the gift of the Holy Spirit is bestowed in its fulness [*sic*] should normally precede admission to participation in the rite which expresses the completeness of Church-membership and of its obligations'. Thus there is a clear sense in this report that initiation is a process and that it is completed in the Eucharist. Within that process additional grace is given through confirmation.[2]

(b) The Lambeth Conference of 1968 encouraged a renewal of the Church and its structures throughout the Communion. This renewal was intended to include greater flexibility about forms of ministry and about the pattern of initiation. There could be certain 'possible lines of experiment'. Confirmation and admission to Holy Communion could be separated in one of two ways. Either a baptized child 'of appropriate age' could receive instruction and be admitted to Communion, with confirmation following later as a commissioning and confirming for the task of being a Christian in the world. Or infants could be baptized and confirmed in a single rite and then admitted to Holy Communion at an early age, after adequate instruction. In due course, when they were 'capable of making a responsible commitment', the bishop would commission the person for service, but this would be an additional rite to that of confirmation.[3]

(c) In the Church of England, the Ely Report on Christian Initiation (1971) was the first official statement to endorse the BACSI position. It rightly pointed out that baptism 'cannot be added to, supplemented, or "completed"', but went on to draw the conclusion (a conclusion that, I would say, does not follow from the premise) that baptism is 'the one and complete sacrament of Christian initiation'. After baptism, there could be no further degrees of initiation: 'it is initiation'. This seems to assume that baptism comprises the totality of initiation, not merely its complete sacramental dimension, so that there is no element of initiation that is not included in baptism.[4] The Ely Report was criticized by the Archbishop of Canterbury, Michael Ramsey; its account of the Anglican tradition on initiation was tendentious.

(d) The 1979 Book of Common Prayer of the Episcopal Church of the USA (ECUSA – now The Episcopal Church) endorsed BACSI. 'Holy Baptism is full initiation by water and the Holy Spirit into Christ's Body the Church' (p. 298). The American Prayer Book attempted to achieve a unified rite, albeit in the context of infant baptism which is resistant to that aim. There is provision for

---

2 *Doctrine in the Church of England (1938): The Report of the Commission on Christian Doctrine appointed by the Archbishops of Canterbury and York*, with an introduction by G. W. H. Lampe (London: SPCK, 1982), pp. 186–9.

3 *The Lambeth Conference 1968: Resolutions and Reports* (London: SPCK; New York: Seabury Press, 1968), pp. 98–9.

4 *Christian Initiation* (London: Church Information Office, 1971), p. 27.

chrismation, administered by a priest, at baptism, and the bishop often gives a second chrismation at 'confirmation'. Confirmation is seen as the first occasion of 'mature public affirmation' (p. 412) of the baptismal commitments made by those baptized at an early age. Some would see this as a reductionist view of confirmation: the emphasis is on the human response, rather than the divine gift – the baptismal promises are affirmed, but what does the Holy Spirit give? The rite may prove helpful and affirming for those who undergo it, but the 1979 Prayer Book created a predicament for American Episcopalians – What exactly is happening in 'Confirmation'? and this has generated intense debate, notably in the pages of the *Anglican Theological Review*. [5]

(e) In 1991 the fourth International Anglican Liturgical Consultation, meeting in Toronto, stated roundly in its report *Walk in Newness of Life*: 'Baptism is complete sacramental initiation and leads to participation in the Eucharist. Confirmation and other rites of affirmation have a continuing pastoral role in the renewal of faith among the baptized but are in no way to be seen as a completion of baptism or as necessary for admission to communion.' One consequence of taking this position on BASCI was that the Consultation also pronounced that 'The pastoral rite of confirmation may be delegated by the bishop to a presbyter.' (Recommendations arising from the various consultations do not have official authority for Anglicans, unless they are subsequently adopted by the Lambeth Conference and/or individual provinces of the Communion.)

(f) The report of a working party of the Church of England's House of Bishops *On the Way: Towards an Integrated Approach to Christian Initiation* (1995) included the findings of the Toronto consultation without comment in an appendix, but explicitly distanced itself from the BACSI position. Initiation is a

---

5 See J. G. Burnett, 'Reconsidering a Bold Proposal: Reflections, Questions and Concerns Regarding a Theology of Confirmation', *ATR* 88.1 (2006), pp. 69–83, which re-affirms BACSI and sees confirmation as an opportunity for the affirmation of faith; K. Tanner, 'Towards a New Theology of Confirmation', *ATR* 88.1 (2006), pp. 85–94, which attempts to retrieve confirmation in the classical sense as a sacrament of strengthening by the Holy Spirit, not simply as an affirmation of faith, but wants to do this without relinquishing BACSI. In my view, these two aims are incompatible. There has also been an intense debate in the pages of the *Anglican Theological Review* about whether, in spite of the clear rules of the Episcopal Church, unbaptized persons should be admitted to Holy Communion as an expression of inclusiveness. See also C. J. Podmore, 'The Baptismal Covenant in the American Church', *Ecclesiology* 6.1 (2010), pp. 8–38. For a reconstructed Episcopal perspective that seems to be broadly in line with the present argument see L. Weil, 'Baptism as the Model for a Sacramental Aesthetic', *ATR* 92.2 (2010), pp. 259–70

'process' and a 'journey'.[6] A report by the House of Bishops in 1996 (GS 1212) treated the traditional sequence of initiation as the norm. It spoke of 'the signs and sacramental acts of Christian initiation' and stressed that baptism was primary and central among these, as the foundation that precedes any other initiatory act. It included the laying on of hands and admission to Holy Communion as 'the two other main elements in initiation'. For the avoidance of doubt it unequivocally re-affirmed the canonical discipline (B 15A) that baptism must always precede admission to Communion (no unbaptized person can lawfully receive Holy Communion in the Church of England). The bishops then went on to accept a variation within the traditional process of initiation, one that would allow baptized, but unconfirmed, children to receive Holy Communion after instruction.

(g) The report of the Formal Conversations between the Methodist Church and the Church of England, that led to the Anglican–Methodist Covenant, treated Christian initiation as a process. It commented that 'in our churches baptism is generally seen as the essential first stage of a process of Christian initiation that includes Confirmation and participation in Communion'. Regarding confirmation, the report recognized that, within the Christian tradition, confirmation has been understood in a variety of overlapping ways. 'Fundamentally, however, as our liturgies show, Confirmation is regarded by both churches as a means of grace within the total process of Christian initiation.' It is seen as a strengthening of the candidate, by the Holy Spirit, for discipleship (paragraphs 122, 126).[7] The Joint Implementation Commission under the Covenant is currently working on questions of initiation and membership.

(h) *Common Worship*, the Church of England's current set of liturgical texts, has not embraced BACSI. The theme of initiation as a process and a sequence is clearly brought out, both in the rite itself and in the commentary. In this respect, it continues the tradition of the Book of Common Prayer (as does the 2004 Prayer Book of the Church of Ireland). A service of confirmation was included in the various successive editions of the BCP from 1549 to 1662. Although it was not regarded as necessary to salvation, confirmation was a vital part of Christian initiation. It was a means of grace that gave strength to resist temptation and to live the Christian life. This provision obviously made

---

6 *On the Way* (London: Church House Publishing, 1995), pp. 93, 107, 108, 118.

7 *An Anglican–Methodist Covenant: Common Statement of the Formal Conversations between the Methodist Church of Great Britain and the Church of England* (Peterborough: Methodist Publishing House; London: Church House Publishing, 2001), pp. 40–1.

sense when virtually all baptisms were of infants. But confirmation was still required in 1662 when for the first time a service of baptism was provided for those who were 'of riper years and able to answer for themselves' (i.e., mainly those who had missed out on baptism during the upheavals of the Civil War and Commonwealth periods, and slaves on the plantations of the early empire). It seems clear, from the requirement that those adults who were baptized should be confirmed by the bishop as soon as convenient, that baptism and confirmation were seen as parts of a process of Christian initiation. Thus there is considerable continuity and consistency in the practice of initiation in the English Church from medieval times, through the Reformation to the present day.

Why has BACSI become widely accepted?

Before offering a critique of BACSI, I think we should ask why it seems to have gathered considerable support. If it is misguided, why is it so widely accepted? Given that it has no official status in the Anglican Communion (it has not been endorsed by a Lambeth Conference and clearly runs against the liturgical tradition stemming from the BCP), why has it made considerable headway among Anglicans? There must surely be more to BACSI than meets the eye. In response to this challenge, I want to explain that I recognize that BACSI embodies certain vital principles, while (I would claim), also tending to distort them.

Baptism is at the heart of Christian initiation

The proponents of BACSI are right to the extent that we cannot take too high a view of baptism or exaggerate its importance. For the sixteenth-century Reformers and their successors, baptism, as the sacrament of our union with Christ, was a momentous event. The fact that it was at that time normally administered only to infants did not detract from its power. The service for the public baptism of infants in the Book of Common Prayer (1662) compares baptism to the ark that kept Noah and his family safe in the flood and to the passing of the children of Israel through the Red Sea. It washes away sins and delivers from God's wrath. In the Catechism that is included in the Book of Common Prayer, 1662, the catechumen answers: 'in my baptism . . . I was made a member of Christ, the child of God, and an inheritor of the kingdom of heaven'. But it does not follow from the truth that baptism is the foundation and heart of initiation that baptism comprises the whole of initiation.

Baptism cannot be repeated

All churches agree that water baptism can be received only once. It is not possible, theologically, to be re-baptized. It is the nature of baptism that it is unrepeatable. Where Baptists appear to 're-baptize' a person who has previously been baptized in infancy, they believe that the candidate is undergoing true baptism for the first time. The unrepeatability of baptism appears to lend some support to the BACSI position, because it suggests the finality of the sacrament. But what is unrepeatable does not necessarily stand alone; it may be part of a larger whole.

Baptism cannot be incomplete or partial

Defenders of BACSI are right to say that baptism cannot be 'completed' or 'topped up' by any other element in Christian initiation. Baptism 'contains', sacramentally, Christ and all that is his: in baptism we receive Christ and all his benefits. The Holy Spirit is the 'milieu' of baptism; baptism is permeated by the Spirit.[8] 1 Corinthians 12.13 (to look no further) seems decisive: it is 'in one Spirit' that we have all been baptized into the Body of Christ. As members of Christ we share his messianic anointing with the Spirit, as Prophet, Priest and King and so are constituted as a royal, prophetic priesthood.[9] This points to the difficulty with the language of 'perfecting' applied to confirmation, used by Richard Hooker and Lionel Thornton CR. What is being 'perfected'? For Hooker, it is the work of grace, begun in us by baptism; for Thornton, it seems to be our vocation as disciples. Neither of these seem objectionable, provided it is not baptism itself that is said to be perfected in confirmation, but perhaps the language is a little unfortunate.[10]

8 Cf. G. W. H. Lampe, *The Seal of the Spirit* (London: Longmans, 1951).

9 See discussion and references in P. Avis, *A Ministry Shaped by Mission* (London and New York: T&T Clark, 2005), pp. 65–9.

10 R. Hooker, *Of the Laws of Ecclesiastical Polity*, V, lxvi, 1: 'to confirm and perfect that which the grace of the same Spirit had already begun in baptism'. Hooker also endorses the language of 'strengthening' in virtue and against temptation (4, 9). L. S. Thornton CR, *Confirmation: Its Place in the Baptismal Mystery* (Westminster: Dacre Press, 1954); Thornton derives the language of 'perfecting' from the Epistle to the Hebrews.

Baptism is normally necessary for salvation

The traditions shaped by the Reformation insist that the conditions of salvation are clearly revealed in Scripture.[11] It has been common ground between the mainstream churches that baptism is normally necessary for salvation. This is taught in both the Lutheran Augsburg Confession of 1530 and the Book of Common Prayer.[12] It is a teaching that can appeal to Scripture in Matthew 28.19; Mark 16.16 (the longer ending); John 3.5 and Acts 2.38. However, as the early Church recognized, this requirement of church discipline needs to be tempered with flexibility. So the early Fathers acknowledged that there could be a baptism of desire and a baptism of blood (i.e. martyrdom), as well as water baptism. In modern times, several churches have reflected on the possibility of those of other faiths being saved through the work of Christ, even though in his life they may have no knowledge of him.[13]

The Reformers did not regard confirmation as a sacrament and therefore as necessary to salvation. Thus they rejected the popular mediaeval belief (though it was not the official teaching of the Western Church) that confirmation or chrism was necessary to salvation.[14] Article XXV of the Thirty-nine Articles lists confirmation as one of the five rites 'commonly called sacraments', while at the same time insisting that confirmation does not have the nature of a sacrament of the gospel, as do baptism and the Lord's Supper. The Homily on Common Prayer and the Sacraments, by Jewel

11 For example Article VI of the Church of England's Thirty-nine Articles of Religion, 1562–71: *Of the Sufficiency of the Holy Scriptures for salvation*: 'Holy Scripture containeth all things necessary to salvation: so that whatsoever is not read therein, nor may be proved thereby, is not to be required of any man, that it should be believed as an article of the Faith, or be thought requisite or necessary to salvation.'

12 For example, Augsburg Confession IX (translation of Latin text): 'Our churches teach that Baptism is necessary for salvation . . . '; BCP, 'A Catechism': the two dominical sacraments are 'generally necessary to salvation'.

13 Vatican 2: *Nostra aetate: Declaration on the Relations of the Church to Non-Christian Religions*: A. Flannery (ed.), *Vatican Council II, vol. 1, The Conciliar and Post-Conciliar Documents* (New York: Costello, 1975), pp. 738–42; Doctrine Commission of the Church of England, *The Mystery of Salvation* (London: Church House Publishing, 1995).

14 *Apology of the Augsburg Confession*: 6. W. Tyndale, Parker Society [PS], I, p. 277; J. Jewel, PS, II, p. 1126: 'They said he was no proper Christian, that was not anointed with this holy oil chrism. This was another abuse. For whosoever is baptized receiveth thereby the full name of a perfect Christian, and hath the full and perfect covenant and assurance of salvation.' See also G. W. Bromiley, *Baptism and the Anglican Reformers* (London: Lutterworth Press, 1953); for the Reformed family of churches, J. W. Riggs, *Baptism in the Reformed Tradition: An Historical and Practical Theology* (Louisville, KY: Westminster John Knox Press, 2002).

[Book II, no. 9] also recognizes a broader, as well as a narrower, definition. Confirmation is not a dominical sacrament, but an edifying ordinance of the Church.

Nevertheless, in the Reformation and post-Reformation periods confirmation is seen as a means of grace, not as a human work, and it meets the first criterion (derived from Peter Lombard) of a sacrament in the Catechism: an outward visible sign of an inward spiritual grace (the second criterion being dominical institution). The BCP sees confirmation as a sacramental action concerned with strengthening the Christian. This view reflects the mediaeval tradition that is also upheld by the Roman Catholic Church. The Second Vatican Council says of those who have been baptized: 'Reborn as sons of God, they must confess before men the faith which they have received from God through the Church. Bound more intimately to the Church by the sacrament of confirmation, they are endowed by the Holy Spirit with special strength' (*Lumen Gentium*: 11).[15]

Christian initiation, including baptism and Holy Communion, should be as unified as possible

Mediaeval and Reformation views of confirmation did not make the connection between baptism, confirmation and the Eucharist as strongly as they might have done. This disjunction gives ammunition to BACSI. There is a theological, if not always a chronological, unity to the rite or rites of initiation. Initiation is the induction of new Christians into the mystical Body of Christ. Although the word 'initiation' is not found in Scripture, initiation is a mystical event, not a sociological phenomenon. Initiation is precisely into the salvation process, that is to say, the process of the reception of God's gift of salvation in Jesus Christ. If baptism is one focal point of the salvation process, the Eucharist is another. Both of the dominical sacraments, baptism and the Eucharist (more correctly, participation in the celebration of the Eucharist and first Communion) take their place within the totality of Christian initiation because both of them induct us into the salvation process, into the mystery of Christ. To make one's communion is the culmination of sacramental initiation, which remains incomplete if this point is not reached. Could one say that a person was fully initiated and inducted into the life and worship of the mystical Body of Christ if that person had never received the sacramental body of Christ? Full

15 W. M. Abbott (ed.), *The Documents of Vatican II* (London and Dublin: Geoffrey Chapman, 1966), p. 28.

participation in the Eucharist, including receiving the sacrament, is a means of grace that completes the process of initiation.[16]

Thus there are several reasons why BACSI has gained credence. What they amount to is the belief that we cannot over-emphasize the importance of baptism. On closer examination, however, these reasons do not demonstrate the truth of the BACSI position. It does not follow from the momentous soteriological significance of baptism that baptism is complete Christian initiation, or even complete sacramental initiation. It is complete as baptism (when it is administered with water, in the threefold divine name, and with the intention to do what the Church does) and the BACSI school of thought is right to affirm this. But that does not mean that baptism is complete as Christian initiation. Initiation requires several elements in addition to baptism, some of them being sacramental. Can we be initiated into Christ and his Body without, in every individual case, young or old, undergoing instruction and teaching about the faith into which we are to be baptized? Does it make sense to say that we have been completely initiated as Christ's disciples if we have not yet had an opportunity publicly to confess our faith in him? Have we received all that God has to give us if we have not received the strengthening of the Holy Spirit for discipleship through the laying on of hands and prayer, following the apostolic pattern? Finally, is it credible to insist that we have been fully and completely initiated into the life of the Body of Christ when we have not participated in the celebration of the Eucharist and, as part of that, received sacramentally his body and blood?

Why is it important to see Christian initiation as a process?

We should not get hung up on the word 'process'

It is sometimes said that initiation is not a process but an event. I am happy to consider initiation as an event, provided we think in terms of an extended or unfolding event, an event that has several stages. When a Shakespeare play is performed, that is an event, but there are several 'acts' and even more 'scenes'

16 Cf. Benedict XVI, Post Synodal Exhortation, *Sacramentum Caritatis* (2007): 'If the Eucharist is truly the source and summit of the Church's life and mission, it follows that the process of Christian initiation must constantly be directed to the reception of this sacrament . . . our reception of Baptism and Confirmation is ordered to the Eucharist. Accordingly, our pastoral practice should reflect a more unitary understanding of the process of Christian initiation . . . The Holy Eucharist, then, brings Christian initiation to completion.'

within the play. When a Beethoven symphony, concerto or sonata is performed, that too is an event, but there are usually several 'movements' within the piece of music. An event may be composite, composed of several parts which are linked together, and it may take place over an extended period. Christian initiation is an extended, articulated event.

The full appropriation of all that is given in baptism requires an extended process

Initiation is a process of receiving, and baptism is the heart and the paradigm of this.[17] No doubt God's whole gift of salvation is contained in baptism (just as it is in the Eucharist), but we need a process, including other sacramental occasions, in order to receive the gift to the full extent. Baptism is an 'effectual' means of grace. It conveys what it signifies. Baptism is the sacrament of rebirth or regeneration by the Holy Spirit, through which the gift of the Spirit is received. We are born into a new relational world. Because baptism makes one a member of the Body of Christ, it is both ontological and relational: in fact, the ontology itself is essentially relational. However, it is equally important to emphasize that baptism requires a human response of faith and of committed discipleship and can be appropriated and entered into again and again, more and more, throughout one's life.

The BCP Catechism's definition of a sacrament ('an outward and visible sign of an inward and spiritual grace given unto us, ordained by Christ himself, as a means whereby we receive the same, and a pledge to assure us thereof') implies that the Anglican doctrine of baptism is philosophically realist. That is to say, the sacrament is not a human theatrical gesture but truly effects what it signifies – provided that the collateral conditions regarding the formal intention are fulfilled (it is not a magical enactment or performance). Baptism is also eschatological in the sense that its meaning and effect are only partially realized in this life: we hope to receive within ourselves the definitive experience of union with Christ at the consummation of God's saving purposes, in heaven. The tension between these two aspects, the realist and the eschatological, can be managed when baptism is seen in personalist and relational terms – its theological import is covenantal. Baptism is a relational transaction in the personal mode. This is what makes baptism one of the foundations of Christian unity.

17 See on this theme S. W. Sykes, *Unashamed Anglicanism* (Nashville: Abingdon Press, 1995), pp. 13ff: Sykes suggestively analyses the themes of reception and divine promise in the BCP service for the baptism of children.

Article XXV of the Thirty-nine stresses that the sacraments do not work automatically, but require appropriate human receptivity: 'And in such only as worthily receive the same they have a wholesome effect or operation: but they that receive them unworthily purchase to themselves damnation, as Saint Paul saith.' The central idea in the Thirty-nine Articles and in Richard Hooker is that baptism is an 'effectual sign', but one that functions only in the context of prayer, faith and the life of the Christian community. There is a tension and a connection – a tensive logic – in the position that affirms both the initiative of grace and the indispensability of human response (even though we know that the human response of faith is enabled by God); that speaks of a God-given effectual sign, but stresses that its effectiveness depends on prayer and faith (even though we know that prayer too is inspired by the Holy Spirit); that has a high biblical view of baptism as union with Christ in his death and resurrection and then applies that to the baptism of those who are not yet old enough to answer for themselves.[18]

Baptism is the focal sacramental event in a process of Christian initiation that includes several vital steps. Though baptism is the pivotal event of this process, other elements are integral to it. As an unfolding process by which the grace of God, decisively and definitively given in baptism, is received and appropriated, Christian initiation is necessarily extended in time, even if certain crucial moments are sometimes compressed together. As St John of the Cross put it, God gives his gift of grace at God's own pace, that is to say, all at once; but we receive that gift at our human pace, little by little. Initiation comprises a journey into Christ and his Church. The initiation is not complete until the journey has been completed and the process has run its full course. In addition to baptism, initiation includes instruction in the faith, personal profession of faith, strengthening for service by the Holy Spirit and admission to Holy Communion. Baptism and the Eucharist are the Alpha and Omega of Christian initiation. The package should be seen as a whole.[19]

The elements that, from a human point of view, make this process fruitful and effective for those who are baptized are faith, prayer and obedience, all qualities that belong to discipleship. But this discipleship is conceived corporately, not individualistically. There is a strong sense of vicariousness, of

18 See the report of the informal conversations between the Council for Christian Unity and the Baptist Union of Great Britain: *Pushing at the Boundaries of Unity* (London: Church House Publishing, 2005).

19 See P. Fiddes, 'Baptism and the Process of Christian Initiation', *Ecumenical Review* 54.1 (2002), pp. 48–65.

'on behalf of'. Christ does for us what we cannot do for ourselves and we as Christians do for our fellows what they cannot yet do for themselves in order that they may eventually perform it. The aspect of 'on behalf of' is perhaps most pronounced when a young child is brought for baptism. The faith, prayer and commitment are those of the parents, the godparents and the congregation as together they hold the child before God. What is contained in a concentrated form in baptism is released, appropriated and received through the total process of Christian initiation.

To think of Christian initiation as process is helpful ecumenically

Although the ecumenical movement has brought about a mutual recognition of baptism between many churches, this is not universal. For some dialogue partners, the Baptists and Pentecostalists, there can be no mutual recognition of baptism because they do not accept infant baptism. What may be possible, and is held out by some Baptist theologians, is mutual recognition of patterns of Christian initiation.[20]

Important ecumenical developments involving Anglicans have been predicated on the recognition of a baptism that is common to each of the partner churches to the dialogue: e.g. the ARCIC report *Church as Communion* (1991), the Meissen Agreement (1991), the Porvoo Agreement (1996), the Reuilly Agreement (1999) and the Anglican–Methodist Covenant (2003). For Anglicans at least, the mutual recognition of baptism is a major stepping stone to mutual recognition and commitment between churches and paves the way for a united mission. As the Second Vatican Council shows, recognition of baptism entails recognizing to some degree the ecclesial reality of those fellowships (at least as 'ecclesial communities' – a Vatican II term that, rightly or wrongly, has been regarded as offensive by Protestants and Anglicans, who insist that they are Churches in the proper sense of the word).[21] It undercuts exclusive ecclesiologies, such as the traditional Roman Catholic and Orthodox positions, that regard one's own church or communion of churches as the only one that contains all the authentic elements of the Church of Christ.

The way forward to some degree of mutual ecclesial recognition for Baptists

---

20 See the conversations referred to in n. 18 and the report of the international conversations between the Baptist World Alliance and the Anglican Communion: *Conversations Around the World* (London: Anglican Communion Office, 2005).

21 *Lumen Gentium* 8, 15; *Unitatis Redintegratio* 22: Abbott (ed.), *The Documents of Vatican II*, pp. 23, 33f; 363f.

and Anglicans may be through the development of a theology of the total process of Christian initiation. This would recognize the unique and indispensable place of baptism within an ongoing process of initiation. That process would need to include the following essential elements, though the order in which they are experienced may vary somewhat:

- baptism with water in the name of the Holy Trinity

- instruction in the faith and formation for discipleship

- a liturgical opportunity for the individual to profess the faith for themselves

- the laying on of hands with prayer for the confirming and strengthening power of the Holy Spirit

- participation in the Eucharist and reception of Holy Communion.[22]

The mutual recognition of processes of initiation by Anglicans and Baptists could not imply any defect in the baptism of infants that would somehow be rectified in arrears by putting in place the other elements of the process: baptism must always be held to be complete as baptism – to that extent BACSI is right. There could be no suggestion that infant baptism was not a true baptism at the time, but could subsequently become recognized as such when supplemented by catechesis, profession of faith, confirmation and Holy Communion. Anglicans could not accept any additional criteria for authentic baptism than the classical criteria of catholic theology: that baptism should be in water, in the Triune Name and with the formal intention of doing what the Church does. The completeness and integrity of the baptism administered to infants could not be called into question, though that would not imply that it comprised complete Christian initiation. In other words, it would have to be seen as complete as baptism (and therefore not to be repeated), though not complete as Christian initiation.

Conclusion

The pragmatic usefulness, in one corner of the ecumenical vineyard, of seeing Christian initiation as a whole process, rather than seeing baptism as complete

---

22 The BCP 1662 takes the baptism of adults very seriously. The rubrics for the service for 'The Public Baptism to such as are of Riper Years and able to Answer for Themselves', echoed in Canon B 24, stress that examination and instruction of the candidates shall take place in good time and that they shall be exhorted to prepare themselves *by prayer and fasting* to receive this sacrament.

sacramental initiation, does not, of course, prove its truth and does not in itself refute BACSI. But it may be, paradoxically, that dialogue with Baptists can help to point us back to the pattern of initiation as it was broadly understood and practised in the Western Church for centuries, is still upheld by the Roman Catholic Church, and is fully and unambiguously reflected in the Anglican tradition running from the BCP to *Common Worship*. With pastoral skill much of the fragmentation of the rite can be overcome, even in the case of those baptized as infants, and disjunction can be avoided. We can have a holistic grasp of Christian initiation within the process approach.

To insist, as I do, that initiation is a process that is centred on baptism, but not confined to baptism, leaves several questions unanswered. In particular, it does not clarify what the nature of the further blessing or gift of the Holy Spirit, imparted at confirmation, is, if the Spirit has been given in baptism. Is it 'strengthening' for discipleship, witness and spiritual conflict, or is it something even more than this, perhaps a fuller participation in the event of Pentecost and a receiving of the sevenfold gifts of the Spirit (Isa. 11. 2–3), as the Anglican liturgies suggest? The BCP rite of confirmation explicitly affirms both the strengthening *and* the sevenfold gifts (as does *Common Worship*, though not quite as explicitly) in the same breath and without seeing any tension between the two. After all, to confirm simply means to strengthen.[23] Surely we should hold both aspects together in our own theology.

However, certain truths about Christian initiation seem clear.

- Christian initiation is a journey, a process, an extended event.

- The Holy Spirit is the agent at work throughout Christian initiation.

- The sacramental dimension of initiation is not exhausted by baptism.

- Confirmation brings a further gift of grace, a strengthening and equipping by the Holy Spirit.

- Initiation cannot be complete until every Christian has had the opportunity to confess the faith for themselves in a liturgical setting, and in the case of those baptized in infancy, to make their baptism promises their own.

23 'The Order of Confirmation' (1662): 'Almighty and everliving God, who hast vouchsafed to regenerate these thy servants by water and the Holy Ghost, and hast given unto them forgiveness of all their sins: Strengthen them, we beseech thee, O Lord, with the Holy Ghost the Comforter, and daily increase in them thy manifold gifts of grace; the spirit of wisdom and understanding; the spirit of counsel and ghostly strength; the spirit of knowledge and true godliness; and fill them, O Lord, with the spirit of thy holy fear, now and for ever.'

Initiation into the life and worship of the Body of Christ comes to completion only at first communion, through participation in the Eucharist, when we are drawn into the movement of Christ's self-offering to the Father, and receive sacramentally his body and blood, his divine life and strength. Then and only then have we been fully inducted into the life of grace that God has provided in the Church. Then and only then are we fully fledged disciples, spiritually equipped and prepared for witness and ministry.

3

Baptism and confirmation – from the New Testament to the Reformation

Martin Davie

Introduction

Is baptism in the Church of England today the same as baptism in the New Testament and the early Church? How did confirmation come about, and does it have any biblical basis? To answer questions such as these, this chapter begins by looking at the theology and practice of baptism in the early Church, as witnessed to by the New Testament. It then traces the development of the theology and practice of baptism during the patristic and mediaeval periods, noting how confirmation emerged as a rite separate from baptism from the end of the patristic period onwards. Finally, it considers the theology and practice of baptism and confirmation developed by the English Reformers in the sixteenth century and reflected in the Thirty-Nine Articles and the Book of Common Prayer (1662).

1. Beginning with Galatians

In his letter to the churches in Galatia sometime around AD 48 or 49 Paul makes what may be the earliest reference to Christian baptism in the New Testament: 'As many of you as were baptized into Christ have clothed yourselves with Christ' (Gal. 3.27). This sudden mention of baptism raises a number of questions.

- Where did the practice of Christians being baptized come from?

- What happened in baptism?

- How is baptism related to the saving work of Christ?

- How is faith related to baptism?

- What is the relationship between baptism and the gift of the Holy Spirit?

2. Jesus' baptism and our baptism

Baptism did not appear out of the blue. Before there was Christian baptism, baptism was administered by John the Baptist and among those baptized by John was Jesus himself. His baptism is the foundation for subsequent Christian baptismal theology and practice.

a) Dying and rising with Christ

The baptism of Jesus in the river Jordan by John is one of the most certain elements of the tradition.[24] The Church would not have invented the story that the sinless Jesus underwent a baptism of repentance for the remission of sins.[25] Although they describe the event slightly differently, all four Gospels record that Jesus was baptized in the river Jordan by John (Matt. 3.13–17; Mark 1.9–11; Luke 3.21–22; John 1.29–34).[26] One of the distinctive things about the baptism of John, compared with other forms of ritual washing practised in first-century Judaism[27] – alongside the fact that it was administered to people rather than self-administered and that it was a once for all rather than a repeatable event – was that it signified a plea to God for the forgiveness of sins in view of the imminent arrival of the Messiah bringing divine judgement. This raises the question of why Jesus was baptized.

The obvious answer would be that Jesus was baptized because he had a sense of personal sinfulness. However, this obvious answer would be at odds with everything else that the Gospels say about Jesus. As G. R. Beasley Murray puts it: 'He who so taught, lived and died, with a moral

24 C. A. Evans, 'Context, family and formation' in M. Bockmuehl (ed.), *The Cambridge Companion to Jesus* (Cambridge: Cambridge University Press, 2001), p. 21.

25 E. Ferguson, *Baptism in the Early Church* (Grand Rapids: Eerdmans, 2009), pp. 99–100. See also R. L. Webb, 'Jesus' Baptism: Its Historicity and Implications', *Bulletin for Biblical Research* 10.2 (2000), pp. 261–309.

26 Although John does not describe the baptism he refers to it. It is also referred to in Acts 1.22, 10.37–38, and 13.24–25. For a discussion of John's baptism and its possible antecedents in Jewish practice see Ferguson, *op. cit.*, Ch. 5 and R. L. Webb, *John the Baptizer and Prophet* (Sheffield: JSOT, 1991).

27 Such as the ritual washings practiced at Qumran and the baptism of converts to Judaism. (what is known as 'proselyte baptism'). For these see Ferguson, *op. cit.*, Ch. 4.

consciousness that did not falter from the baptism to the cross, was assuredly not baptized as a sinner seeking mercy of the Judge; if it was for sins, it was for sins not His own.'[28]

If the sins for which Jesus was baptized were not his own then whose were they? The answer that is given to us by the Gospels and by the New Testament as a whole is that as the promised Messiah Jesus was called to live out the vocation of the Suffering Servant of the Lord described in Isaiah 40–55 and as such was called to identify with the fate of a sinful Israel and a sinful world and to suffer for their salvation. In the three Synoptic Gospels the voice that speaks from heaven declares 'This is my Son, the Beloved, with whom I am well pleased' (Matt. 3.17; cf. Mark 1.11; Luke 3.2). The voice addresses Jesus in a composite quotation from Scripture (Ps. 2.7; Isa. 42.1). Psalm 2 proclaims the accession of the anointed king, who is to rule the nations with a rod of iron. Isaiah 42.1–6 is the first of a series of prophecies about the Servant of the Lord, who has been chosen to carry the true religion to the Gentiles and who, in achieving this mission, must suffer indignity, rejection and death.[29]

Matthew describes an exchange between Jesus and John about Jesus' desire for baptism: 'Then Jesus came from Galilee to John at the Jordan, to be baptized by him. John would have prevented him, saying, "I need to be baptized by you, and do you come to me?" But Jesus answered him, "Let it be so now; for it is proper for us in this way to fulfil all righteousness." Then he consented' (Matt. 3.13–15). The key phrase in these verses is Jesus' statement that 'it is proper for us in this way to fulfil all righteousness'. Righteousness was an important concept for Matthew. It often refers to God's saving activity, but here it probably means to obey God's plan. In receiving baptism Jesus identified with the people of Israel to whom John addressed his message, and started on the path that led to the cross (Matt. 16.21–23).[30]

In the Fourth Gospel, Jesus' baptism is prefaced by John's declaration, 'Here is the Lamb of God who takes away the sin of the world.' Jesus is baptized as the one who will offer himself as a sacrifice on behalf of the world. His baptism at the hands of John reveals his identity with sinners as the ultimate sacrificial

---

28 G. R. Beasley Murray, *Baptism in the New Testament* (Exeter: Paternoster Press, 1972), p. 47.

29 Cf. G. B. Caird, *St. Luke* (Harmondsworth: Pelican, 1971), p. 76.

30 Ferguson, *op. cit.*, p. 102. See also the discussions in R. T. France, *Matthew* (Leicester: IVP, 1985), pp. 94–5; O. Cullmann, *Baptism in the New Testament* (London: SCM Press, 1958), pp. 16–22.

lamb, who fulfils the Passover sacrifice, the morning and evening sacrifices in the Temple and the prophecy of Isaiah 53.1–12.[31]

Additional material in the Gospels which illuminates the meaning of Jesus' baptism is contained in Mark 10.38–40 and Luke 12.50, both of which refer to a baptism with which Jesus is and will be baptized. We can see three aspects to these references to baptism. First, there is obedience: 'Just as Jesus had submitted to complete immersion in the Jordan in obedience to his Father's will and as a pledge of further obedience, so at some time during his ministry he began preparing himself to be "obedient to death," to make his whole body an offering on the cross.'[32] Secondly, there is cleansing. John's baptism was a rite of cleansing and Jesus' baptism/death was likewise connected with cleansing, but 'the purpose of his submission to death was not cleansing for himself but cleansing for the world'.[33] Thirdly, there is new life. Seen in the light of the other predictions about Jesus' fate contained in the Gospels the 'accomplishment' of baptism (Luke 12.50), to which Jesus looks forward, is not simply his death but also his resurrection.[34]

If we bring together what is said in all the passages from the Gospels looked at thus far we find three things. (i) Jesus' 'baptism' refers both to the baptism that he underwent at the hands of John the Baptist in the River Jordan and also to the 'baptism' of his death and resurrection. The first points to and leads to the second. (ii) Jesus' baptism means his vicarious suffering for sinners. As the Anglican–Reformed international report *God's Reign and Our Unity* puts it: 'Jesus, the sinless one, went down into the waters of Jordan in solidarity with our sinful race, submitting vicariously to the judgement of God upon guilty sinners. The coming judge was the man judged for sinners . . . '[35] (iii) Jesus' baptism speaks not only of his death but also of his resurrection; as an integral part of his mission to fulfil God's purposes as described in Isaiah 40–55, his resurrection as well as well as his suffering must be vicarious. Just as he dies to cleanse people from sin, so he rises to give them new life. 'We have been buried with him by baptism into death, so that, just as Christ was raised from

31 See E. Hoskyns and F. N. Davey, *The Fourth Gospel* (London: Faber and Faber, 1949), p. 176; Pope Benedict XVI, *Jesus of Nazareth* (London: Bloomsbury, 2007), pp. 20–2.

32 E. R. Burrows, 'Baptism in Mark and Luke', in S. E. Porter and A. R. Cross (eds), *Baptism, the New Testament and the Church* (Sheffield: Sheffield Academic Press, 1999), p. 111.

33 *Ibid.*, p.111.

34 *Ibid.*, p.113.

35 *God's Reign and Our Unity* (London and Edinburgh: SPCK/St Andrew's Press, 1984), pp. 30–1.

the dead by the glory of the Father, so we too might walk in newness of life' (Rom. 6.1–11). In Romans 6.3 Paul asks the Romans rhetorically, 'Do you not know?' Paul's assumption suggests that belief that baptism into Christ involved baptism into his death belonged to the earliest Christian teaching.[36] The likelihood that Paul's teaching in Romans 6 reflects existing Christian tradition is increased by the fact that there is more general evidence that his teaching was rooted in the testimony about Jesus accepted in the Church as a whole.[37]

If we go on to enquire where this tradition came from, the most likely explanation is that it was based on the life and teaching of Jesus himself.[38] If we accept the tradition reflected in Matthew 28.19 that the risen Jesus commanded his followers to baptize, then the most plausible explanation for the origin of the early Christian view of baptism was that Jesus not only taught them to baptize but instructed them as to the meaning of baptism. As Alan Richardson says, if we ask where the 'wholly new conception of baptism as an act of incorporation into the resurrection-body of the crucified Messiah' came from, the most convincing explanation is that it was Jesus himself who first taught that his own death was a baptism that must be shared by all who would participate in the messianic salvation.[39]

A related idea to that of dying and rising with Jesus is the idea of baptism as putting on Christ and therefore putting off the old nature. We have already

36 C. E. B. Cranfield, *Romans*, Vol. I (Edinburgh: T&T Clark, 1985), p. 300.

37 See, for example, D. Wenham, *Paul: Follower of Jesus or Founder of Christianity?* (Grand Rapids: Eerdmans, 1995). In Colossians 2.12, 'Paul' is able to assume that the Colossians share the belief that baptism means dying and rising with Christ, and in 1 Corinthians 15.29 in which, as part of his attempt to persuade the Corinthians of the physical nature of the resurrection, Paul asks the Corinthians why, if there is no resurrection, they undergo baptism on behalf of the dead. What precisely is meant by baptism for the dead continues to be debated, but the logic of Paul's argument demands that both he and the Corinthians share a common belief that baptism and resurrection go together and the most obvious reason for this is that a link between baptism and resurrection was a generally accepted part of the faith of the early Church as a whole. See A. C. Thiselton, *The First Epistle to the Corinthians* (Grand Rapids: Eerdmans, 2000), pp. 1240–9.

38 For the idea that the traditions of early Christianity were rooted in what the Church knew to be the life and teaching of Jesus himself see C. H. Dodd, *The Apostolic Preaching and its Developments* (London: Hodder and Stoughton, 1944); and R. Bauckham, *Jesus and the Eyewitness* (Grand Rapids: Eerdmans, 2006).

39 A. Richardson, *An Introduction to the Theology of the New Testament* (London: SCM Press, 1958), p. 339.

seen this idea in Galatians 3.27 and it is also found in Colossians 2.11 and seems to be in the background in Romans 13.14, Colossians 3.9–10 and Ephesians 4.22–24. In Colossians 2.11–14 the idea of putting off the old nature is juxtaposed with the idea of dying and rising with Christ, and the notions of putting off the old nature and putting on the new and dying and rising with Jesus overlap with each other in that they both point to the notion of baptism leading to a new way of being that needs to be reflected in a new way of behaving.

It has been suggested that the imagery of putting off the old nature and being clothed with/putting on Christ originated in the fact that the early Christians were baptized naked and therefore took off their clothes before being baptized and put them on again afterwards.[40] This may indeed have been the case. However, direct evidence for this is lacking and the metaphor of being clothed is very common in the Old Testament (see Job 8.22, 29.14, 39.19; Ps. 35.26, 93.1, 104.1), and elsewhere in the New Testament where there is no evidence of a literal clothing being in the background (Luke 24.29; Acts 1.8).

In Galatians 3.26–27 Paul binds faith and baptism together 'as two aspects of entering into Christ. One now belongs to Christ on the basis of faith in him by being baptized into him.'[41] Richardson comments that 'in the church of the New Testament, faith and baptism belong together, like soul and body in biblical thought: the one cannot exist without the other . . . to believe means to obey'.[42]

b) Receiving the Holy Spirit

A second key aspect of baptism that goes back to the baptism of Jesus himself is receiving the Holy Spirit. In their accounts of Jesus' baptism, all four Gospels describe the Spirit descending on Jesus. The accounts differ slightly between the Gospels. Matthew 3.16 and Mark 1.10 describe Jesus as seeing the Spirit descending on him like a dove after he has come up out of the water. Luke 3.21–22 notes that it was as Jesus was praying that the Spirit descended and suggests that the Spirit's descent was visible to others. John 1.32 describes the baptism indirectly via the testimony of John the Baptist. It is silent about when the Spirit descended like a dove, but stresses that the Spirit not only descended on Jesus, but remained on him, making him someone permanently endowed

40 *Ibid.*, p. 151.
41 Ferguson, *op. cit.*, p. 147.
42 Richardson, *op. cit.*, p. 348.

with the Spirit. However, in spite of these differences, all four accounts agree on the central fact that the Spirit descended on Jesus in the context of his baptism.

The Synoptic Gospels also present John the Baptist as teaching that someone was coming after him who would baptize people with the Holy Spirit (Matt. 3.11; Mark 1.8; Luke 3.16) and John's Gospel makes explicit what is implicit in the Synoptics when it links the descent of the Spirit on Jesus with his ability to baptize others with the Spirit: 'He who sent me to baptize with water said to me, "He on whom you see the Spirit descend and remain, this is he who baptizes with the Holy Spirit"' (John 1.33).

This verse establishes the link between our baptism and Jesus' baptism. Just as Jesus' baptism was the point at which the Spirit descended and remained on him, so also at our baptism he gives the Spirit to us and thereby enables us to share in his relationship with the Father, a relationship that was affirmed by a voice from heaven at his baptism (Matt. 3.17; Mark 1.11; Luke 3.22; cf. John 1.34).

> The Christ who was himself baptized for us in our humanity by the Holy Spirit in the Jordan, who was baptized in blood for us on the cross, to secure our sonship, at Pentecost baptized the church by the same Spirit to make it his Body in a corporate baptism. And he still baptizes us personally into union with himself by the Spirit of adoption whereby we too, by a shared baptism of the Spirit, can cry; '*Abba*, Father.'[43]

Five important images used in the New Testament to describe the effect of the gift of the Spirit at baptism are the images of washing, sealing, anointing, sonship and new birth.

Washing

Saul of Tarsus was instructed by Ananias, 'Rise and be baptized, and wash away your sins, calling on his name' (Acts 22.16). The connection between the outward use of water in baptism and an inward cleansing from sin is clear here, and a similar connection is also made in Ephesians 5.25–27 and Hebrews 10.22–23. In these three texts there is no mention of the Holy Spirit, but a connection between being cleansed from sin in baptism and the work of the

---

43 J. B. Torrance, *Worship, Community and the Triune God of Grace* (Carlisle: Paternoster, 1996), p. 68.

Spirit is made in two other texts. In 1 Corinthians 6.9–11 Paul lists different types of wrongdoing that are a bar to inheriting the kingdom of God and which used to be characteristic of some of those to whom he is writing, but he then goes on to say: 'You were washed, you were sanctified, you were justified in the name of the Lord Jesus Christ and in the Spirit of our God.' 'In the name of the Lord Jesus' is an allusion to the baptismal confession or possibly a baptismal formula and the reference to the Holy Spirit describes either the Spirit's role of cleansing or sanctifying through the water, or the gift of the Spirit at baptism.[44]

In Titus 3.3–7 Paul writes: God 'saved us . . . through the water of rebirth and renewal by the Holy Spirit'. The world translated 'water' by the NRSV is literally 'washing', so here we have the same idea of the washing away of sin in baptism by means of the action of the Holy Spirit that we have already seen in 1 Corinthians 6.[45]

A further passage which refers to washing in the context of baptism is 1 Peter 3.20–21. After describing how Noah and his family were 'saved through water at the time of the flood', the passage continues: 'And baptism, which this prefigured, now saves you – not as a removal of dirt from the body, but as an appeal to God for a good conscience, through the resurrection of Jesus Christ.' The idea of baptism as washing is clearly in the background here, but the author wants to make clear that baptism is not about the removal of physical uncleanness but rather constitutes 'an appeal to God for a good conscience'. Colwell argues that the word translated 'conscience' refers to 'self-consistency before God, the mark of a character that is integrated with gospel'.[46] In relation to this passage this means that: 'The significance of baptism lies in the orientation of life to God through the resurrection of Christ.' [47]

---

44 Ferguson, *op. cit.*, p. 150.

45 For the details of the interpretation of this passage see Ferguson, *op. cit.*, pp. 162–4. A. Thiselton notes in *The Hermeneutics of Doctrine* (Grand Rapids: Eerdmans, 2007, pp. 536–8) that scholars such as James Dunn and William Mounce have questioned whether there is a reference to baptism in these passages. However, R. Schnackenburg, *Baptism in the Thought of St. Paul* (Oxford: Blackwell, 1964), pp. 3–17, and Ferguson, *op. cit.*, pp. 149–50, 161–4 and pp. 187–8, continue to defend the traditional view.

46 συνειδήσεως: J. E. Colwell, 'Baptism, Conscience and the Resurrection: A Reappraisal of 1 Peter 3.21', in Porter and Cross, *op. cit.*, p. 216.

47 *Ibid.*, p. 218.

Sealing

There are three passages where, it is generally agreed, we find the idea of Christians being sealed by the Spirit in baptism:

- 2 Corinthians 1.22: 'he has put his seal upon us and given us his Spirit in our hearts as a guarantee.'

- Ephesians 1.13–14: 'In him you also, who have heard the word of truth, the gospel of your salvation and have believed in him, were sealed with the promised Holy Spirit which is the guarantee of our inheritance until we acquire possession of it, to the praise of his glory.'

- Ephesians 4.30: 'And do not grieve the Holy Spirit of God, in whom you were sealed for the day of redemption.'

It is also probable that the idea of baptism as sealing is meant in Revelation 7.3–8 where John describes the hundred and forty four thousand that were 'sealed' 'out of every tribe of the sons of Israel'.

What sealing means in these passages is that 'Christians in their baptism receive the internal mark or sign of the Holy Spirit; this "mark" is not accessible to human inspection in this age, but is nevertheless the sign by which those who belong to God will be recognized in the day of judgement.'[48]

Underlying the use of sealing to refer to baptism is the rabbinic idea, based on Genesis 17.9–14, that circumcision was the divinely appointed sign or seal of a person standing within the covenant made by God with Abraham, an idea which lies behind Paul's argument in Romans 4.11 that circumcision was a sign of Abraham being justified by faith. For Paul, as Colossians 2.11–12 makes clear, baptism is the Christian equivalent of circumcision: 'In him also you were circumcised with a circumcision made without hands, by putting off the flesh in the circumcision of Christ; and you were buried with him in baptism, in which you were also raised with him through faith in the working of God, who raised him from the dead.' The 'circumcision of Christ' seems to be an image for his death on the cross.

Given that Paul views baptism as the Christian equivalent of circumcision, it is not surprising that he adapts rabbinic terminology by referring to the work of the Spirit in baptism as a seal. What marks people off as belonging to God's new covenant community is not the outward sign of circumcision, which

48 Richardson, *op. cit.*, p. 351. For the idea of baptism as sealing see also Beasley Murray, *op. cit.*, pp. 171–7.

applied only to Jewish males, but the inward work of the Spirit given through baptism which is something for everyone, whether they are male or female, Jewish or Gentile.[49] We do not know whether, in the Church of the New Testament period, there was some external sign, such as, for instance, marking with the sign of the cross, to show that Christians had been sealed by God.

Anointing

The image of anointing is found in four passages.

- Acts 10.38: 'God anointed Jesus of Nazareth with the Holy Spirit and with power.'

- 2 Corinthians 1.21: '. . . it is God who established us with you in Christ and has anointed us . . .'

- 1 John 2.20 and 27: because Christians have been 'anointed by the Holy One' they know all truth.

The image of anointing refers back to a number of Old Testament passages. The Kings of Israel were anointed and became *meshiah Yahweh*, the Lord's anointed (1 Sam. 16.13, Ps. 89.20, 2 Kings 9.3). The priests were also anointed for their office (Ex. 29.7, 40.13–15; Lev. 8.12; Ps. 132.2) and, most importantly of all, the Isaianic prophet was anointed with the Spirit of the Lord (Isa. 11.2, 42.1, 44.3, 61.1). So also, Jesus, as the messianic Prophet, Priest and King, is anointed with Spirit of the Lord at his baptism to fulfil his threefold calling. The same is true of all who share in Jesus' baptism and ministry. That is why in The Acts those who have received the Spirit carry out the same ministry that we see Jesus performing in Luke's Gospel: his ministry is continuing in them through their anointing by the Spirit.

Was there a literal anointing with oil at baptism in New Testament times? Scholarly verdicts vary. A liturgical anointing at baptism may have been practised. The evidence is consistent with such an anointing, but does not require it.[50]

---

49 See Romans 2.28–29 and Galatians 3.27–29. For a detailed study of the idea of sealing see G. W. H. Lampe, *The Seal of the Spirit* (London: Longmans, Green and Co., 1951).

50 Beasley Murray, *op. cit.*, p. 233; Cullmann, *op. cit.*, Ch. iv; Richardson, *op. cit.*; L. Mitchell, *Baptismal Anointing* (London: SPCK, 1966), p. 16, referring to G. Dix, 'Confirmation, or Laying on of Hands?', *Theology*, Occasional Papers No. 5, 1936; and L. S. Thornton, *Confirmation, its Place in the Baptismal Mystery* (Westminster: Dacre Press, 1954); T. W. Manson, 'Entry into Membership of the Early Church,' *Journal of Theological Studies*, Vol. 48, 1947, pp. 25–33.

Sonship

As we saw at the beginning of this paper, in Galatians 3 and 4 St Paul links becoming a child, literally a 'son', of God with baptism and with the gift of the Spirit that leads Christians to cry 'Abba Father'. As Ferguson notes, 'the sequence is not that the Spirit comes to make persons children of God but that because they are children they receive the Spirit. They become children because they are in Christ, the Son. And they enter into Christ at baptism.'[51]

The same sequence can also be seen in Paul's argument in Romans 6–8. In Romans 6.1–11 Paul describes how in baptism Christians participate in the dying and rising of Jesus. In Romans 6.12–23 he then goes on explain that this means that Christians need to lead lives that reflect the fact that they have been set free from sin. In Romans 7 Paul argues that the Jewish law cannot enable people to live in this way, but then in Romans 8.1–2 he picks up the main thread of his argument, stating that 'There is therefore now no condemnation for those who are in Christ Jesus. For the law of the Spirit of life in Christ Jesus has set you free from the law of sin and death.' The idea of baptism is still in the background of the Apostle's argument here. Through baptism Christians are united to Christ, and as such they partake of the Holy Spirit who sets them free from the law of sin that leads to death.

The same idea is also in the background in Romans 8.14–17. As those who have become children of God through their baptism into Christ, Christians possess the 'Spirit of adoption' and this Spirit leads them to cry 'Abba Father' as a witness that they are indeed children of God.

New birth

In John 3.5 Jesus says to Nicodemus: 'Very truly, I tell you, no one can enter the kingdom of God without being born of water and Spirit.'

Traditionally this passage has been seen as reference to baptism and in the second century it was in fact the most frequently cited text regarding baptism.

There are scholars who question whether there is a baptismal reference in this verse and who see the reference to water as either a way of referring figuratively to the Spirit or as a description of human conception or birth.[52] But there probably is a reference to baptism in this verse, because it follows on

---

51 Ferguson, *op. cit.*, p. 147.

52 See for example D. A. Carson, *The Gospel according to John* (Grand Rapids: Eerdmans, 1991), pp. 191–206.

from the testimony of John the Baptist in John 1.33 and links up with the references to baptism that follow (John 3.22–26 and 4.2). Furthermore, if water is simply a reference to the Spirit, it is difficult to explain why the Spirit is mentioned in two separate ways in one verse and the idea that water refers to human conception or birth is also difficult given that grammatically John 3.5 refers to one birth not two. In John 3.5 there is one birth, the birth from above that involves both water and the Spirit, and a reference to baptism seems to be the obvious meaning.[53]

As Ferguson observes, as a reference to baptism, John 3.5 'provides a combination of the ideas of baptism, sonship (new birth) and the presence of the Holy Spirit' that we also find in St Paul's theology of baptism.[54] What we do not find in John is the idea of putting on Christ or dying and rising with Christ, although the idea of the believer being united with Christ is certainly present in John (see John 15.1–11), and the Spirit by whom Christians are re-born at baptism is the Spirit of the 'glorified' Christ (John 7.39), that is the Christ whose death on the cross is simultaneously his exaltation by God. That is why in John's account of the crucifixion the dying Jesus gives up his spirit (John 19.30) which can be seen simply as a reference to Jesus breathing his last, but is better understood as a Johannine play on words and as a reference to Jesus giving his Spirit to the faithful disciples gathered around the cross.[55]

We have seen that the significance of baptism is described in a variety of different ways in the New Testament. What gives coherence to this varied picture, however, is that all the different ways of understanding baptism ultimately link back to Jesus' own baptism by John in the Jordan. They relate to the two key ideas of participating in the dying and rising of Jesus on our behalf and being endowed with the same Spirit who descended on Jesus at his baptism, so that we can share in Jesus' relationship with the Father and in his messianic ministry.

3. Baptism and becoming a member of the Church

For Paul the fundamental promise by God that gives meaning to the story of Israel in the Old Testament is the promise in Genesis 12.3 that God will give Abraham offspring through whom the nations of the world will be blessed.

---

53 See Ferguson, *op. cit.*, pp. 143–5.
54 *Ibid.*, p.145.
55 Hoskyns and Davey, *op. cit.*, p. 530.

The argument that Paul develops from Galatians 3.1 onwards is that this promise to Abraham (Gal. 3.8) is fulfilled in Jesus (Gal. 3.16) and that Christians receive the promised blessing through faith by being baptized and thereby putting on Jesus and receiving his Spirit.

It is because baptism is both the means and the mark of belonging to this new community that it is described as the Christian circumcision. Furthermore, the fact that Christians are part of God's covenant people is also a fundamental part of their being children of God through baptism. In Galatians 3.1–4.7 Paul holds the ideas of Christians being children of God and their being the heirs of Abraham together. As those who have put on Jesus, Christians are children of God, but given that Jesus is also the heir promised to Abraham, Christians are therefore also the heirs of the promise to Abraham and collectively God's covenant people.[56]

In the new community that we enter at baptism differences of race, class and sex are transcended (Gal. 3.26–29). The same truth is expressed in the image of the body and its members: 'For just as the body is one and has many members, and all the members of the body, though many are one body, so it is with Christ. For by one Spirit we were all baptized into one body – Jews or Greeks, slaves or free – and all were made to drink of one Spirit' (1 Cor. 12.12–13). The Body of Christ is the Church. It is in the Body of Christ/the Church that the Corinthians have received the Spirit and the gifts of the Spirit, and Paul's argument in 1 Corinthians 12.1–14.38 is that as those baptized into the one body the Corinthians need to learn to exercise these gifts in humility, harmony and love.[57]

4. Baptism and the Spirit in The Acts of the Apostles

On the day of Pentecost the Spirit descended on the Apostles and those who were with them in accordance with Jesus' promise to them before his

---

56 It is the same idea of the fulfilment of God's promises to Abraham that also underlies Paul's argument in Romans (see N. T. Wright, *Paul: Fresh Perspectives* (London: SPCK, 2005)). In Ephesians Paul paints the same picture on an even bigger canvas. He takes the story back to God's eternal plan to unite all things on heaven and earth in Christ (Eph. 1.10), but he still sees the Church, as a community made up of both Jews and Gentiles, as central to God's purposes, and his argument in 2.11–22 seems to reflect the baptismal theology that he develops in his other letters even though baptism itself is not mentioned.

57 For the interpretation of 1 Corinthians 12.12–13 see Thiselton, *op. cit.*, pp. 995–1001. In Colossians 2.8–4.1 Paul develops the implications of baptism for the life of the Church in a similar fashion.

ascension. They began to speak in other tongues and, in response to the crowd's bewilderment about the significance of this, Peter made the connection between the outpouring of the Spirit and the life, death, resurrection and ascension of Christ. Those who heard Peter's sermon were 'cut to the heart' and asked, 'Brothers what shall we do?' Peter's answer was 'Repent, and be baptized every one of you in the name of Jesus Christ for the forgiveness of your sins; and you shall receive the gift of the Holy Spirit' (Acts 2.37–38). Peter's answer has generally been seen as outlining the two key elements of Christian baptism: the forgiveness of sins through participation in the dying and rising of Christ, and the gift of a new relationship with God through the Spirit (Acts 2.16–21; Joel 2.28–32).

The third element of baptism, becoming part of the Church, is implicit in what comes next in the Book of Acts, Luke's description of how those who were baptized formed a new community which was marked by devotion to 'the apostles' teaching and fellowship, to the breaking of bread and the prayers' and by a community life in which goods and possessions were held in common (Acts 2.41–47).

Although Acts 2.38 has generally been seen as linking the gift of the Spirit with baptism, the question has been raised about whether such a link can be seen in the Book of Acts as a whole. This is because there are three other texts which appear to separate baptism and the gift of the Spirit.

1.   In Acts 8.4–17 Philip brings the gospel to Samaria and, in response to his preaching and the miraculous signs that he performs, men and women are baptized, but they do not receive the Spirit until Peter and John arrive and lay hands on them.

2.   In Acts 10.44–48 Peter is preaching to the Gentile centurion Cornelius and his household when the Spirit falls upon them and they start praising God in tongues. Peter draws the conclusion that those who have received the Spirit cannot be refused the gift of baptism.

3.   In Acts 19.1–7 Paul encounters some 'disciples' at Ephesus who were baptized into John's baptism and have not heard of the Holy Spirit. Paul baptizes them in the name of Jesus and lays hands on them and they receive the Spirit and speak in tongues and prophesy.

Two conclusions have been drawn from these three passages.

●   Luke (and perhaps also the early Church more widely) were simply not concerned about the relationship between baptism and the gift of the Spirit. Christians needed to be baptized and they needed to have the Spirit, but it did not really matter whether the Spirit was received before, during or after baptism.[58]

- In the early Church baptism with water for the forgiveness of sins and the gift of the Spirit were two different events with the latter taking place through the laying on of hands.

Closer examination of the three passages concerned indicates, however, that both of these arguments are precarious.

First, all three passages assume that the link between baptism and the gift of the Spirit set out in Acts 2.38 is 'the pattern and norm for entry into the Church'.[59] In Acts 8 the reason why Peter and John lay hands on the Samaritans is precisely because the Spirit that ought to have come upon the Samaritans at their baptism has not done so. In Acts 10 the fact that the Spirit who is given through baptism has been given to Cornelius and his household indicates that they are people who can properly be baptized even though they are Gentiles. In Acts 19 it is the fact that the disciples have not received the Holy Spirit that leads Paul to enquire about the nature of their baptism, presumably on the grounds that if they had received Christian baptism they ought to have received the Spirit.[60]

Secondly, in none of these passages is Luke concerned with the relationship between the use of water or the laying on of hands and the gift of the Spirit. In Acts 8 and 10 his concern is with the fulfilment of Jesus' promise in Acts 1.8 that they would be his witnesses 'in Jerusalem and in all Judea and Samaria and to the end of the earth'. Acts records how this began to take place from the day of Pentecost onwards and as it took place the issue inevitably arose as to whether first Samaritans and then Gentiles could be part of the people of God.

---

58 See, for example, J. D. G. Dunn, *Unity and Diversity in the New Testament*, 2nd edn (London: SCM Press, 1990), pp. 154–7.

59 K. W. Noakes, 'Initiation – From New Testament Times until St. Cyprian', in C. Jones, G. Wainwright and E. Yarnold (eds), *The Study of Liturgy* (London: SPCK, 1980), p. 84.

60 In Acts 18.25 St Luke's description of Apollos could mean that he was someone who was 'fervent in spirit' (RSV) or 'spoke with burning enthusiasm' (NRSV) which is the majority view, or it could mean that he was fervent 'in the Spirit' even though he had only received the baptism of John. If it means the latter, it would seem that in his case John's baptism had become Christian baptism through belief in Jesus and receipt of the Spirit. In this case too, however, the link between baptism and the Spirit would be maintained. A proper baptism is one that results in the gift of the Spirit.

In Acts 8 and 10 we find this question answered by both the action of the Apostles and the action of God. In Acts 8 Peter and John lay on hands and God sends down the Holy Spirit. In Acts 10, by contrast, God sends down the Holy Spirit and Peter baptizes. In both cases, however, there is a dual authorization of the inclusion of those previously outside the people of God.[61] In Acts 19 Luke's concern is to underline, as he has already underlined in his Gospel (Luke 3.16), the difference between John's baptism and Christian baptism, the difference being that at Christian baptism the Spirit is given to those who are baptized.

It may be the case that Acts 8 and Acts 19 reflect the fact that from the earliest days of the Church the laying on of hands with prayer for the gift of the Spirit was an integral part of baptism and this may also be what is referred to in Hebrews 6.2 when it refers to both 'ablutions' and the 'laying on of hands'. If this was the case it would explain why the laying on of hands in baptism seems to have been a very widespread practice in the Church during the Patristic period.[62]

5. Baptism and confession of faith

In the 'Western' text of the Book of Acts we find an additional verse in 8.37. To the Ethiopian eunuch's question, 'What is there to stop me being baptized?', Philip replies, 'If you believe with all your heart you may.' And the eunuch responds, 'I believe that Jesus Christ is the Son of God.' This variant reading points us to the idea of baptism being preceded by some form of confession of faith.

There are no other explicit accounts in Acts or elsewhere in the New Testament of baptism being preceded by a confession of faith. However, Romans 10.9, 'If you confess with your lips that Jesus is Lord and believe in your heart that God raised him from the dead, you will be saved,' has generally been taken as referring to a confession of the lordship of Christ at baptism. The baptismal confession of Jesus as Lord presumably also lies behind baptism 'in the name of

---

61 A good comparison would be with Acts 15 where the decision about whether the Gentiles needed to be circumcised is made by the apostles and elders but is based on the action of God in sending the Holy Spirit as recorded in Acts 15.9–10. See also J. B. Green, 'From "John's Baptism" to "Baptism in the Name of the Lord Jesus"; The Significance of Baptism in Luke-Acts', in Porter and Cross, *op. cit.*, p. 172.

62 Although it was very widespread it was not universal. In some places the laying on of hands gave way to chrismation.

the Lord Jesus' in Acts 8.16 and 19.5 and in 1 Corinthians 6.11 and the confession 'Jesus is Lord' in texts such as 1 Corinthians 12.3 and Philippians 2.11.[63] An alternative form of confession may have been the confession 'Jesus is the Son of God' which occurs in Acts 8.37 and is also referred to in 1 John 4.15 and 5.5 and in the account of Peter's confession of faith at Caesarea Philippi in Matthew 16.15.[64]

Although there are no explicit accounts of catechetical activity in preparation for baptism in the New Testament, fragments of catechetical material may be preserved in passages such as Romans 1.3–4; 1 Corinthians 8.6, 15.3–8; 1 Timothy 3.16; and 1 Peter 3.18–22, which give concise summaries of the basics of the Christian message, and may also underlie Philippians 2.6–11.[65]

6. Infant baptism

For most of the history of the Christian Church the baptism of infants has been the normal practice. However, there is a continuing debate about the propriety of this practice, a debate which has two aspects, one historical and the other doctrinal.

The historical question is whether the baptism of infants took place in New Testament times. There is clear evidence for the baptism of infants from the end of the second century onwards. The question is what happened before then.

The different answers to this question are well illustrated by the debate that took place between Kurt Aland on the one hand and Joachim Jeremias on the other in the early 1960s. Aland argued that infant baptism was an innovation that took place around 200 AD. He held that before then the Church saw no need to baptize infants and baptized people only at a time when they were able to exercise conscious faith. He contended that the baptism of households referred to in Acts 11.14, 16.15, Acts 16.31–33 and 1 Corinthians 1.16 and 16.15 would have involved adult members of the household, including slaves, but would not have included infants. He also contended that there was no clear evidence for the practice of infant baptism prior to 200.[66]

---

63 J. N. D. Kelly, *Early Christian Creeds*, 3rd edn (Harlow: Longman, 1972), p. 15.
64 *Ibid.*, p. 16.
65 *Ibid.*, pp. 16–21.
66 K. Aland, *Did the Early Church Baptize Infants?* (London: SCM Press, 1962).

Jeremias argued that the practice of infant baptism went back to the earliest days of the Church. The language used about baptism in the New Testament reflects the Jewish practice of the baptism of proselytes and this indicates that the Church continued the Jewish practice of baptizing the children of adult converts. This is presupposed in the references to the baptism of households. The words, 'do not stop them' (μὴ κωλύετε) in Mark 10.14 reflect the language of the baptismal liturgy, and the story of the blessing of children by Jesus in Mark 10.13–15 reflects the baptismal practice of the Roman church at the time that Mark wrote. The evidence of second-century figures such as Polycarp (*Martyrdom of Polycarp* 9), Justin (*I Apology* 15.6), Irenaeus (*Against Heresies* 2.22.4), and early third-century figures such as Hippolytus (*Apostolic Tradition* 21), Origen (*Commentary on Romans* 6.5–7) and Tertullian (*De Baptismo*) provide a chain of evidence that takes the practice of infant baptism back to apostolic times.[67]

As Thiselton notes, the doctrinal aspect of the debate is concerned with the 'hermeneutics of what baptism means'.[68] On the one hand there are those who hold that at the heart of baptism as described in the New Testament there has to be a conscious human response to what God has done for us in Jesus. Thus Karl Barth declares that 'the meaning of baptism is man's conversion – the conversion of all who have a part in it. It is the conversion that takes place in knowledge of the work and word of God. It is the common forsaking of an old way of life and the common following of a new way of life.'[69] On this basis Barth argued that the practice of infant baptism was illegitimate.

On the other hand, his fellow Reformed theologian Pierre Marcel argued that infant baptism is legitimate because it reflects the priority of divine grace to which faith is a response, reflects the parallel effectiveness of word and sacrament in mediating divine grace and corresponds to the biblical pattern of covenant and covenant signs.[70]

The Church of England has traditionally held that the historical evidence for the practice of infant baptism from New Testament times is persuasive and

---

67 J. Jeremias, *Infant baptism in the First Four Centuries* (London: SCM Press, 1960) and *The Origins of Infant Baptism; A Further Study in reply to Kurt Aland* (London: SCM Press, 1963).

68 Thiselton, *op. cit.*, p. 514.

69 K. Barth, *Church Dogmatics*, IV.4, 1969, p. 138.

70 P. Marcel, *The Biblical Doctrine of Infant Baptism, Sacrament of the Covenant of Grace* (London: James Clarke, 1954).

that the practice bears witness to the provenience of grace and the continuity between the covenant signs in the Old and New Testaments.[71]

7. Baptism in the Patristic period

There is continuing scholarly debate about the development of baptismal rites during the Patristic period.[72] The evidence that we have is limited and susceptible of different interpretations. However, what does seem clear is as follows:

- The earliest accounts of baptism outside the New Testament – chapter 7 of the Didache and Justin Martyr's First Apology 61 and 65 – describe a baptismal rite that is preceded by fasting, consists of baptism with water in the threefold name and leads to admission to the Eucharist. There is no mention of any post-baptismal laying on of hands. The same is also true of what Irenaeus says about baptism in *Against Heresies* and in the *Demonstration of the Apostolic Teaching*.

- However, at the end of the second century and the beginning of the third we find in the writings of Tertullian and Hippolytus reference to a rite in which baptism with water is followed by the laying on of hands, with reference being made to Acts 8 and Acts 19, and in Tertullian the giving of the Spirit is seen as taking place through the laying on of hands.[73] The evidence of Tertullian and Hippolytus is significant because it reinforces the idea that from the earliest times baptism may have been a complex rite including both the water and the laying on of hands after the apostolic pattern in Acts.[74] From that point onwards the laying on of hands/

71 See, for example, E. C. S. Gibson, *The Thirty Nine Articles* (London: Methuen, 1908), pp. 635–9; E. J. Bicknell, *A Theological Introduction to the Thirty Nine Articles* (London: Longmans, 1947), pp. 473–7; G. Kuhrt, *Believing in Baptism* (Oxford: Mowbray, 1987).

72 See, for example, M. E. Johnson, *Rites of Christian Initiation: their Evolution and Interpretation* (Collegeville: Liturgical Press, 1999); A. Kavanagh, *Confirmation: Origins and Reform* (New York: Pueblo, 1988); K. B. Osborne, *The Christian Sacraments of Initiation: Baptism, Confirmation, Eucharist* (New Jersey: Paulist Press, 1987); E. Yarnold, *The Awe Inspiring Rites of Initiation*, 2nd edn (Edinburgh: T&T Clark, 1994).

73 Tertullian, *De Baptismo*, Ch. 8; St. Hippolytus, *The Apostolic Tradition*, Ch. 22.

74 R. Beckwith and A. Daunton-Fear, *The Water and the Wine* (London: Latimer Trust, 2005), pp. 54–5: 'Whilst formally it may be true that, up to and including the time of Irenaeus, no contemporary initiation rite is mentioned apart from baptism in water, this cannot tell the whole story. That from a hitherto simple rite, suddenly, in the first years of the third century there sprang (through the reading of the Book of Acts) an initiation procedure

anointing after baptism becomes standard in the West, and in the East post-baptismal anointing appears from the third century and becomes general by the fifth century.[75]

● In the later Patristic period, while there was no single agreed rite of Christian initiation,[76] there was, in the West at least, a broadly similar overall pattern with many common elements.[77] This pattern involved a period of catechetical instruction followed by testing, prayer and fasting, and then a vigil, sometimes night-long, at the cathedral church (normally on Holy Saturday or the Eve of Pentecost). Following the vigil the candidates renounced evil, and made a profession of faith (this profession of faith is what lies behind the Apostles' and Nicene Creeds) and they were then baptized in water in the name of the Trinity by the presbyters assisted by the deacons (women deacons for women candidates in some places). This would often take place in a separate baptistery. In some places there were anointings by a presbyter after the baptism with water and either after these, or directly after the baptism, the candidates were led to the bishop who completed the rite with a prayer for the sevenfold gifts of the Spirit of Isaiah 11.2, accompanied by the laying on of hands and/or anointing with the oil of chrism.

In the later Patristic period the term 'baptism' was used to refer to this series of events understood as a single complex whole. It is important to note this when

---

of considerable complexity is quite incredible. Irenaeus himself was quite familiar with Acts, and Tertullian and Hippolytus appear to be setting forth, in the main, already established baptismal procedures. It is then much more reasonable to conclude that, as Tertullian could use the term 'baptism' of a complex of rites, so could earlier writers. For them, sometimes at least, 'baptism' or 'the water' was probably shorthand for a developing initiation rite, the elements of which varied somewhat in different parts of the Church.'

75 There is also evidence for pre-baptismal anointing in some of the early Syriac rites, but this did not become standard practice in the Church as a whole.

76 For example, the rites used in Milan and Northern Italy were different from those used in Rome and the rites in Gaul, Spain and Ireland were different again.

77 E. Yarnold, 'Initiation – The Fourth and Fifth Centuries', in C. Jones, G. Wainwright and E. Yarnold (eds), *The Study of Liturgy* (London: SPCK, 1985), p. 95: 'The individual ceremonies that made up the rites of initiation were put together in different orders in different localities, and these individual ceremonies were performed in different ways with different interpretations; nevertheless many of these individual ceremonies remained recognizably the same everywhere.'

the claim is made that in the early Church baptism was complete sacramental initiation. What was meant by 'baptism' was not simply baptism with water, but all the elements of the rite together. This baptismal rite led immediately within the same liturgy to a celebration of the Eucharist at which the newly baptized received Holy Communion for the first time.[78]

In the patristic period there is overall agreement about the basic nature of baptism, an agreement that is built on the biblical teaching that we have looked at.

- Baptism is the work of God that is based on the saving effects of Jesus' death and resurrection.

- Baptism has saving significance and is almost always necessary to salvation. The major exception was the case of martyrs who had died for their faith prior to receiving baptism – they had undergone a 'baptism of blood'.

- Baptism is the circumcision of the heart in contrast to the outward circumcision of the Jewish rite.

- The fundamental blessings of baptism are forgiveness of sins and the gift of the Holy Spirit, sharing in the death and resurrection of Christ and a re-birth from above resulting in adoption as a child of God and the restoration of the divine image.

- Other images that are commonly used to describe baptism are clothing with Christ, enlightenment,[79] marriage to Christ,[80] deliverance from Satan,[81] and a contract involving renunciation and confession of faith.[82]

Two areas of baptismal theology saw significant development in the later patristic period. First, the development in the West of the idea that baptism is necessary for infants in order to deliver them from the effects of original sin, an idea that is found in the anti-Pelagian writings of Augustine and Jerome.[83] This

---

78 For a convenient compilation of the documentary evidence for the baptismal rites in the Patristic period see E. C. Whitaker, *Documents of the Baptismal Liturgy*, 3rd edn (London: SPCK, 1970); Johnson *op. cit.*

79 Hebrews 6.4.

80 Ephesians 5.22–27.

81 Colossians 1.13.

82 I Peter 3.21. For details on the Patristic understanding of baptism see F. Bovon, 'Baptism in the Ancient Church', *Sewanee Theological Review*, 42, 1999, pp. 429–38; Ferguson, *op. cit.*, pp. 201–816; J. N. D. Kelly, *Early Christian Doctrines*, 5th edn (London: A&C Black, 1980).

83 Kelly, *ibid.*, pp. 429–30.

idea was to be fundamental to the thinking about the significance of baptism and the necessity of infant baptism in the Western Church until recent times. Second, the idea that the Holy Spirit was bestowed in the anointing with chrism by the bishop after baptism (with or without the laying on of hands), an idea that can be found, for example, in Hilary, Gregory of Nyssa and Cyril of Alexandria among others.[84] This second development eventually found expression in the theology of confirmation.

8. The emergence of confirmation

Three significant developments took place that led to changes in the pattern of initiation as a complex but unified rite that we have just described.

First, infant baptism became the norm. The pattern described above was based on the premise that those who wished to become Christians were normally adults who were able to answer for themselves. However, as the Christian faith became more established and widely accepted, the practice of Christian parents bringing infants to baptism continued to grow until the majority of those who were baptized were infants rather than adults. This meant that the traditional pattern of catechesis prior to baptism and personal confession of faith at baptism ceased to be viable in the case of most of those who were being baptized. The pattern that replaced it was one in which the personal confession of faith and commitment at baptism was undertaken by parents and godparents on behalf of infants on the understanding that these infants would receive catechetical instruction as they grew up and would then be able to confess the faith for themselves (although this confession of faith was not linked to a rite of confirmation until the Reformation).

Secondly, in the West the growth of infant baptism led to a breaking of the direct link between baptism and admission to the Eucharist. Admission to Communion was postponed until the infants who had been baptized were old enough to receive the sacrament with a proper degree of understanding.

Thirdly, with the growth of the Church in Western Europe from the fifth to the eleventh centuries and the large size of Western dioceses, particularly north of the Alps, it became impractical for all the baptismal rites to be presided over by the bishop in person.

These developments eventually led to the unified rite described above being divided into two. Except in the rare cases of conversion from Judaism or Islam,

---

84 *Ibid.*, pp. 432–6.

a priest administered water baptism to infants soon after they were born. The final part of the rite was then performed by a bishop at some convenient later point in time, initially before children were eight years old but at some stage when the infants had reached the age at which they could answer for themselves.

The existence of this second rite of initiation is widely attested by the turn of the first millennium and from the eleventh century the term confirmation came to be used to describe it (although the term only came to be universally used following the Council of Trent in the sixteenth century). In the West in the Middle Ages there were thus two rites of Christian initiation, baptism and confirmation, the latter rite being obligatory for the faithful though not officially necessary for salvation.

The 'formal' elements of the confirmation rite were determined as prayer by the bishop over the candidates, the anointing of candidates on the forehead, and the laying on of hands and signing with the cross – though increasingly the 'matter' of the sacrament was focused in the anointing with chrism by the bishop.[85]

The dominant mediaeval understanding of the separate rite of confirmation reflected the teaching of the fifth-century Gallic bishop Faustus of Riez that the laying on of hands following baptism strengthened Christians to live the Christian life.[86]

Because confirmation had become a chronologically separate rite from baptism, with a theological significance that was distinct from that of baptism, it came to be regarded in the Middle Ages as being a sacrament in its own right. There were thus two complementary sacraments of Christian initiation, baptism and confirmation.

The pattern that developed in the West in the Middle Ages was for priests to baptize and bishops to confirm. The role of the bishops was justified by reference to the action of the apostles in Acts 8.4–7, the bishops being understood as the descendants of the apostles in this regard.

---

85 Cf. G. Cameron, 'The Development of Confirmation and its relationship to Admission to Communion', in J. Conn, N. Doe and J. Fox (eds), *Initiation, Membership and Authority in Anglican and Roman Catholic Canon Law* (Cardiff and Rome: The Centre for Law and Religion Cardiff University/ Pontifical Gregorian University/ Pontifical University of St. Thomas Aquinas), p. 74.

86 Text in P. Turner, *Sources of Confirmation, from the Fathers through the Reformation* (Collegeville: the Liturgical Press, 1993), pp. 35–6.

It was known, however, that in the East there was a different pattern of initiation in which there was no separate confirmation, but in which those who were baptized were 'chrismated' with the use of chrism blessed by a bishop. In 1351 Pope Clement VI recognized this practice as equivalent to Western confirmation and stated that the See of Rome could give permission for a priest to administer confirmation using chrism prepared by the bishop. The teaching of his decree was reiterated by the Council of Florence[87] and the same idea was also taught by Thomas Aquinas.[88] At the end of the medieval period the Council of Trent anathematized those who denied that the bishop was the ordinary minister of confirmation,[89] but deliberately did not condemn the idea that a priest might act as an *extra*ordinary minister of confirmation.

Because of the close theological connection between baptism and confirmation, children were confirmed in infancy in medieval Europe.

> Both English and Continental councils through the medieval period tried to limit the time which may be allowed to elapse between the rites – legislating for a maximum period of two, three or seven years between Baptism and Confirmation. The Synod of Worcester (1240) decreed that parents who neglected to have their child confirmed within a year after birth should be forbidden to enter the church. The Synod of Exeter (1287) enacted that children should be confirmed within three years from birth, otherwise the parents were to fast on bread and water until they complied with the law.[90]

The difference between the ages specified in these two Synods is indicative of the trend in the Middle Ages towards a later age for confirmation, because bishops were not readily available and confirmation was not seen as vital because (unlike baptism) it was not necessary for salvation. Eventually, the age of confirmation stabilized at seven years old, but the practice of confirming infants when a bishop was available persisted throughout the

---

87 'We read that sometimes for a reasonable and really urgent cause, by dispensation of the apostolic see, a simple priest has conferred this sacrament of confirmation with chrism prepared by a bishop.' Council of Florence, Session 8, text in http://www.ewtn.com/library/COUNCILS/FLORENCE.HTM.

88 St. Thomas Aquinas, *Summa Theologiae*, III.72.11.

89 Council of Trent, *Canons on Confirmation*, Canon 3. 'If anyone says that the ordinary minister of holy confirmation is not the bishop alone, but any simple priest, let him be anathema.' Text in J. H. Leith, *Creeds of the Churches*, rev. edn (Oxford: Blackwell, 1973), p. 429.

90 Cameron, art. *op. cit.*, p. 74.

Middle Ages. The future Queen Elizabeth I, for example, was baptized and confirmed at three days old in 1533, a bishop being readily available at the royal court.

During the Middle Ages there was a continuing debate about the relationship between the three sacraments of baptism, confirmation and Holy Communion. It was accepted, in line with Christian practice from the earliest times, that baptism had to precede admission to Holy Communion, but there was discussion about whether confirmation had to precede Holy Communion as well.

In England Archbishop Pecham decreed at the Council of Lambeth in 1281 that no one should be admitted to Communion before they were confirmed. This regulation seems to have been aimed at bolstering confirmation by giving people an incentive to have their children confirmed. In line with this regulation, the rubric of the Manual of Sarum Rite declared that 'no one must be admitted to the sacrament of the body and blood of Christ save in danger of death, unless he has been confirmed or has been reasonably prevented from receiving the sacrament of confirmation'.[91]

9. The English Reformation

Baptism

Like their patristic and mediaeval predecessors the English Reformers of the sixteenth century believed on the basis of John 3.5 that baptism was 'generally necessary for salvation'[92] and also like them – and like most of the Reformers on the continent – they retained the practice of infant baptism despite the objections that were raised against it by radical Protestant groups. They had two primary reasons for doing so.

First, they believed that there was a straight continuity between circumcision as commanded in Genesis 17 and baptism. As the Elizabethan Dean of St Paul's, Alexander Nowell, puts it in his *Catechism*: 'Seeing God, which never swerveth from truth, nor in anything strayeth from the right way, did not exclude infants in the Jewish church from circumcision, neither ought our infants to be put back from baptism.'[93] Second, they believed that infant

91 *Ibid.*, p. 74.

92 See the description of the sacraments in the Catechism in the Book of Common Prayer and the opening words of its service for the Publick Baptism of Infants.

93 G. E. Corrie (ed.), *Nowell's Catechism* (Cambridge: Parker Society/CUP, 1843), p. 209.

baptism was mandated by the story of the blessing of infants by Jesus in Mark 10.13–15. In the service for the Publick Baptism of Infants in the Book of Common Prayer, for example, this is the set lesson and the Priest then explains how this mandates the infant baptism that is about to be performed :

> Beloved, ye hear in this Gospel the words of our Saviour Christ, that he commanded the children to be brought unto him; how he blamed those that would have kept them from him; how he exhorteth all men to follow their innocency. Ye perceive how by his outward gesture and deed he declared his good will toward them; for he embraced them in his arms, he laid his hands upon them, and blessed them. Doubt ye not therefore, but earnestly believe, that he will likewise favourably receive this present Infant; that he will embrace him with the arms of his mercy; that he will give unto him the blessing of eternal life, and make him partaker of his everlasting kingdom.

How did the English Reformers understand baptism? Drawing on the New Testament and the Fathers, they used a variety of different images to explain its significance. Thus Article XXVII describes the significance of baptism in terms of a new birth, grafting into the Church, the forgiveness of sin and adoption as sons of God: 'Baptism is . . . a sign of regeneration or new birth, whereby, as by an instrument, they that receive baptism rightly are grafted into the Church; the promises of the forgiveness of sin, and of our adoption to be the sons of God, by the Holy Ghost are visibly signed and sealed; faith is confirmed, and grace increased by virtue of prayer unto God.'

The opening prayer in the service for the 'Publick Baptism of Infants' draws on the stories of Noah, the crossing of the Red Sea and the baptism of Jesus in the Jordan (praying that the child 'may be received into the ark of Christ's Church; and being stedfast in faith, joyful through hope, and rooted in charity, may so pass the waves of this troublesome world, that finally *he* may come to the land of everlasting life') in support of the idea that baptism is about deliverance from the wrath of God through the washing away of sin and sanctification by the Holy Spirit so that the person baptized may eventually come to everlasting life.

As Article XXVII also indicates, the English Reformers took an 'instrumental' view of baptism. That is to say, they believed that baptism delivered the benefits that it signified. This is a point that is emphasized by Nowell in his *Catechism*: baptism '. . . hath the truth of the things themselves joined and knit unto it. For as in baptism God truly delivereth us forgiveness of sins and newness of life, so do we certainly receive them. For God forbid that we should think that God mocketh and deceiveth us with vain figures.'[94]

Confirmation

The English Reformers retained a number of elements of the understanding and practice of confirmation that had developed in the Western Church. These were:

- A rite of confirmation that was distinct from the rite of baptism.

- Baptism being performed by a priest and confirmation being performed by a bishop.

- The idea of confirmation as strengthening. Archbishop Cranmer's first confirmation rite of 1549 used the words 'send down . . . thy Holy Ghost', but in 1552 he changed this to 'strengthen them . . . with the Holy Ghost' and it was the 1552 language that was used in the definitive 1662 version of the Book of Common Prayer.

- The mediaeval English discipline of insisting that confirmation should be the normal pre-requisite to receiving Holy Communion.

However, they also departed from the accepted understanding and practice of confirmation in three ways.

First, in line with continental Reformers such as Luther and Calvin the English Reformers rejected the idea that confirmation is a sacrament. This was because it had not been instituted by Christ himself and because they felt that the idea that it was a sacrament had led to an undervaluing of the importance of baptism.[95]

Secondly, again in line with the practice of the continental Reformation, they introduced a new catechetical element into confirmation. In the Middle Ages the Church had sought to ensure that children who were baptized would be brought up to know at least the basic elements of the Christian faith including the Lord's Prayer, the Ten Commandments and the Creed,[96] but children did not answer for themselves at confirmation. The English Reformers however,

---

94 *Ibid.*, p. 208.

95 Cf. *ibid.*, p. 211.

96 See for example E. Duffy, *The Stripping of the Altars* (New Haven and London: Yale University Press, 1992), Ch. 2.

like their continental counterparts, mistakenly believed that in the early Church those baptized as infants were catechized before being brought to a bishop for confirmation.[97] They sought to restore this practice by insisting that no one should be confirmed unless they could say the Creed, the Lord's Prayer and the Ten Commandments and answer the other questions from the Prayer Book Catechism and they made the personal profession of faith an integral part of the confirmation rite. This also meant that the age of confirmation was increased to the early teens, since the emphasis was no longer on getting children confirmed as soon as possible after baptism, but on people only coming to confirmation once they had sufficient knowledge and spiritual maturity to confess the faith for themselves.

Thirdly, in the 1549 Prayer Book the use of the oil of chrism at confirmation was discontinued and the 1552 Prayer Book talked about the bishop laying his hand on the head of the person being confirmed without mentioning signing with the cross (although signing with the cross continued and was the form that hand laying took in some places).

A summary of how the English Reformers wanted confirmation to operate and how they understood its significance is provided by the Preface to the confirmation rite in the 1552 Prayer Book. What comes across very clearly in this Preface is the combination of the two elements of confirmation. Confirmation is described as both a catechetical rite in which those confirmed 'ratify and confirm' the promises made for them at baptism and also a rite in which through the gift of the Spirit given through the imposition of hands and prayer they receive 'strength, and defence against all temptations to sin, and the assaults of the world and the Devil'. Confirmation thus involves both divine activity and human response together.

The Preface also assures people that delaying confirmation until the early teens would not put their children's salvation in peril because 'it is certain by God's word, that children, being baptized, have all things necessary for salvation, and be undoubtedly saved'.

To return to where we began this chapter, at the heart of Christian initiation is dying and rising with Christ and, in consequence, receiving the gift of the Holy Spirit, and what this means for the believer is a life that is marked by faith and repentance. The great strength of the understanding of baptism and confirmation put forward by the English Reformers was that in line with their

---

97 Corrie, *op. cit.*, pp. 210–11.

commitment to justification by faith they stressed the importance of faith and repentance in relation to baptism and showed how this was compatible with continuing to baptize infants.

Nowell declares that what he calls the 'use of baptism' (that is to say, the proper human response to God's activity) consists in two things. First, he says, we must 'with assured confidence hold it determined in our hearts, that we are cleansed by the blood of Christ from all filthiness of sin, and so be acceptable to God, and that his Spirit dwelleth within us.' Secondly, we must continually 'travail in mortifying our flesh, and obeying the righteousness of God, and must by godly life declare to all men that we have in baptism as it were put on Christ, and have his Spirit given us'.[98] Only if we respond in this way will baptism be fruitful in bringing us to eternal life.

As Nowell goes on to observe, this explanation of what baptism involves inevitably leads to the question of why infants are baptized since they are not in a position to live in this way. His response, which reflects the position of the English Reformers as a whole, is that faith and repentance are only required prior to baptism 'in persons so grown in years, that by age they are capable of both'. In the case of infants 'the promise made to the Church by Christ, in whose faith they are baptized, shall for the present time be sufficient'. However, when they have reached an age at which they are capable of doing so, they must then acknowledge for themselves 'the truth of their baptisms, and have the force thereof to be lively in their souls, and to be represented in their life and behaviours'.[99]

What the English Reformers saw, and what the Church of England has continued to see, is that as well as being the occasion on which candidates receive the seven-fold gifting of the Holy Spirit to strengthen them to live the Christian life, confirmation also provides a focus for catechetical activity designed to help people to understand the significance of their baptism as their entry into the life of the Triune God and an opportunity for those who have been baptized as infants to publicly acknowledge what happened to them at their baptism and publicly commit themselves to participating in the life of the Triune God by living as Christ's disciples in the fellowship of his Church in the strength the Spirit provides.

The English Reformers were mistaken historically in thinking that a pattern of Catechesis for those baptized as infants was practised in the early Church.

98 *Ibid.*, p. 209.
99 *Ibid.*

Where they were not wrong was in thinking that such catechesis is desirable and that confirmation provides a helpful focus for it. It was the addition of this catechetical element that was the English Reformers' distinctive contribution to the development of confirmation in the Church of England. However, this did not mean that they saw confirmation as a purely catechetical rite. As we have said, for them confirmation was a rite that involved both human and divine activity. On the human side there was confession of faith and personal commitment to living God's way and on the divine side there was the strengthening gift of the Holy Spirit to make living this way possible.

4

Baptism in the journey of Christian initiation

Harriet Harris

The passage out of slavery

The king in Jesus' parable of the unmerciful slave (Matt. 18.23–35) cancels the slave's impossibly huge debt. He thereby renders irrelevant the whole process of record-keeping and pay-backs. In effect, he dies to the world of calculation and control, and takes his slave with him. They are both dead to that world. It needn't affect them anymore. They are free of it. The slave thereby passes over from debt to freedom, death to life, because of what the king has done to him.

When we die with Christ, it is like dying with the king to debt, sin and the world of slavery, and rising to the new life of freedom, forgiveness and the reign of God. Baptism is our passage out of slavery, when we are brought through the waters of baptism, as the Israelites were brought through the waters of the Red Sea, into freedom and the promised land (cf. 1 Cor. 10.1–4).

> By baptism, Christians are immersed in the liberating death of Christ where their sins are buried, where the 'old Adam' is crucified with Christ, and where the power of sin is broken. Thus those baptized are no longer slaves to sin, but free. Fully identified with the death of Christ, they are buried with him and are raised here and now to a new life in the power of the resurrection of Jesus Christ, confident that they will also ultimately be one with him in a resurrection like his (Rom. 6.3–11; Col. 2.13, 3.1; Eph. 2.5–6) (BEM, para B3).[100]

So baptism is a sacrament of salvation – the passage out of slavery and into

---

100 'BEM' being the landmark paper of the Faith and Order Commission of the World Council of Churches, on *Baptism, Eucharist and Ministry*, Faith and Order Paper No. 111, 1982.

new life. It does not need repeating. The Passover itself is complete, even for those who, like the Israelites in the Wilderness, forget what God has done or were infants at the time. To repeat baptism is to misunderstand and undermine its givenness and its once-for-all nature – which reflect the once-for-all givenness of Christ.[101] Baptism is 'primarily a witness to the saving work of God and only secondarily a witness to our faith, itself a gift of God'.[102] As attested by all but Zwingli and the heirs of the Radical Reformation, baptism is something God does to us.[103] The effective cause of baptism is the Triune God.[104] The Spirit takes us into the exchange between the Father and Son. Therefore, baptism does not depend for its reality (for its truly being our death and resurrection) upon personal faith, however mature that faith may be – except that, like the king in the parable, God does not foist his action upon us but waits for our plea (or a plea made on our behalf).[105]

But while no one needs to be re-baptized, all need to live out their baptism if it is to be fulfilled. The unmerciful slave in Jesus' parable does not realize his freedom, and so it remains unfulfilled.[106] He reverts to the usual pattern of

101 *On the Way: Towards an Integrated Approach to Christian Initiation* (London: Church House Publishing, 1995), p. 27.

102 Martin Reardon's discussion paper, *Christian Initiation: A Policy for the Church of England* (London: Church House Publishing, 1991), p. 45.

103 Zwingli understands sacrament as our doing a visible sign in response to an invisible grace. He does not regard the sign as efficacious, although he does regard it as signifying something that God effects. See Huldrych Zwingli, 'On Baptism', in G. W. Bromiley (ed.), *Zwingli and Bullinger*, The Library of Christian Classics, vol. 24 (Nashville: Westminster John Knox Press, reprint 1973); Huldrych Zwingli, *Commentary on True and False Religion*, ed. Samuel Macauley Jackson (Durham: Labyrinth Press, reprint 1981), p. 182. As he moved towards his death, Zwingli moved more towards an instrumental understanding of baptism. His distinctive emphasis, however, that baptism is something that we do, and particularly that it is a sign of belonging to the Church, has been influential, particularly for the ways in which churches relate baptism to church membership (as discussed later). See Huldrych Zwingli, 'Notes on Refuting Baptist Tricks', in Samuel Macauley Jackson (ed.), *Selected Works* (Philadelphia: University of Pennsylvania Press, 1901).

104 Aquinas, *ST* III, Q. 66 a. 5. Cf., from his different understanding of sacrament, Martin Luther: 'To be baptized in God's name is to be baptized not by men but by God himself; although it is performed by men's hands it is nevertheless truly God's act', Theodore G. Tappert (trans. and ed.) *The Book of Concord: The Confessions of the Evangelical Lutheran Church* (Philadelphia: Fortress Press, 1959), p. 437.

105 Cf. Alexander Schmemann, *Of Water and the Spirit: A Liturgical Study of Baptism* (Crestwood, NY: St Vladimir's Seminary Press, 1974), p. 68.

106 In the parable he loses his freedom and the debt is reinstated. We must not push the analogy between baptism and the parable of the unmerciful slave further than Scripture will

calculation, control and violence, and in particular the violence that he knows as an oppressed slave. He shows no mercy to his fellow slave, probably not because he is unusually mean, but because he is carrying on as he is used to, doing the usual things, living out the normal behaviours and according to the normal expectations of the slave culture in which he has been formed.

The waters of baptism, as Gregory of Nyssa and Cyril of Jerusalem suggest, are for us both tomb and Mother.[107] In them we die to the demands and patterns of this world that have shaped us, and we are born again. In our new life we try to remember and live worthily of our freedom, rather than falling back into the old ways we learned as slaves.

Baptism is also a sacrament of initiation, by which we become members of the Body of Christ. It marks our incorporation into Christ: into his death and resurrection (Rom. 6. 3–11);[108] and into the people who now form the Body of Christ on earth (cf. 1 Cor. 12.12–13; Gal. 3. 27–29) (cf. BEM nn. 1 and 2).

These two roles of baptism, as sacrament of salvation and of initiation, are wholly bound up with one another. Being incorporated into Christ is the means of our salvation. In him and through him we become children of the Father and in communion with the Godhead: 'By the sacrament of baptism a person is truly incorporated into Christ and into his church and is reborn to a sharing of the divine life.'[109]

Membership as incorporation

Any comprehensive order of baptism must contain the declaration that 'the persons baptized have acquired a new identity as sons and daughters of God, and as members of the Church' (BEM, n. 20). As well as entry into the divine life, we acquire new relationships, as brothers and sisters of one another, on account of what Christ has done to us. Dietrich Bonhoeffer writes:

---

bear, but might nonetheless ask whether the harsh ending of the parable reflects the NT churches' immense difficulty with the problem of post-baptismal sin (Heb. 6.4–8, 10.26–31; I John 1.7–9, 3.9). We will take up this problem, and its resolution in the Eucharist, later in the paper. Ecumenically, churches seek to discern in themselves and in one another the extent to which they are living out their baptism.

107 Gregory of Nyssa, *Catechetical Oration* no. 5; Cyril of Jerusalem, *Mystagogical Catechesis*, II.4: 'at the same moment you died and were born – and that saving water was both your grave and your mother'; cf. Schmemann, *op. cit.*, p. 67.

108 Jesus spoke of his own death as a baptism: Mark 10.38; Luke 12.50.

109 Pontifical Council for Promoting Christian Unity, *Directory for the Application of Principles and Norms of Ecumenism* (Vatican City, March 1993), n. 92.

> Without Christ we should not know God and could not call upon him, nor come to him. But without Christ we would also not know our brother, nor could we come to him. The way is blocked by our own ego. Christ opened up the way to God and to our brother. Now Christians can live with one another in peace; they can love and serve one another; they can become one. But they can continue to do so only by way of Jesus Christ. Only in Jesus Christ are we one, only through him are we bound together.[110]

The reality of our membership of Christ and his Church 'is not an ideal which we must realize', but 'rather a reality created by God in Christ in which we may participate'.[111] Living out our membership is the ethical outworking of our baptism. Our relationships are transformed as we make our passage out of the culture of slavery, as we die to sin (Rom. 6) and make room for Christ and for one another.

Confusion over the language of membership

Theologically, the notion of membership helpfully extends the metaphor of the Church as the Body of Christ: bodies have members, and those who are baptized become members of Christ's Body. This is what 'incorporation' means.[112] Baptism is 'the sacrament of membership of the body of Christ (though not into any particular denomination)'.[113]

However, sociologically, the terminology of membership raises complications. The link between baptism and committed membership has weakened in most churches. Not all baptized persons are active members of churches, and not all regulars in church are baptized. It is a pastoral concern whether unbaptized sympathizers can and should be treated as members of the Church. Baptist churches which practise 'open membership', for example, receive members on 'profession of faith' and commitment to the church's life, without insisting on baptism.[114] There are other specific churches where unbaptized persons

---

110 D. Bonhoeffer, *Life Together* (London: SCM Press, 1954), p. 12.

111 *Ibid.*, p. 18.

112 'In Baptism we are made members of Christ', C.R. Bryant, 'Holy Baptism', in *Christian Religion Explained* (London: A.R. Mowbray and Co., 1960), p. 76.

113 P. Avis, *The Identity of Anglicanism: Essentials of Anglican Ecclesiology* (London/NY: T&T Clark, 2008), p. 11, point 8.

114 Contrast 'closed membership', in which baptism by immersion of a believer is a necessary prerequisite for membership. See S. Mark Heim, 'Baptismal Recognition and the Baptist Churches', in M. Root and R. Saarinen (eds), *Baptism and the Unity of the Church*

have been counted as members by other criteria.[115] In short, the notion of membership is vague, as is the status of persons who seem neither to be simply within or without the Church. Some churches, notably those that do not practice infant baptism, have modified accounts of membership to manage these ambiguities.[116]

The ambiguity over language of membership stems partly from differences between traditions over whether or not baptism is a sacrament. Where baptism is understood in Zwinglian terms, as a visible sign that we make in response to an invisible grace, then baptism is not itself efficacious. It is something that we do in response to an invisible efficacy worked within us. Baptism, under this understanding, can be performed by ministers as a mark of entry into a community. Incorporation into the Body of Christ, on such a non-sacramental understanding, can be understood to have happened over a period of time. Baptism is then performed at a particular time, as a sign that this is so.

Entry and initiation

Baptism is initiatory in the basic sense that it is our entry into new life in Christ. Thomas Aquinas regarded it as the most necessary sacrament because it is the 'door' or 'gateway' to all the others,[117] while the Eucharist is the most glorious

---

(Grand Rapids/Geneva: Eerdmans/WCC, 1998), pp. 159–60, and John E. Colwell, *Promise and Presence: An Exploration of Sacramental Theology* (Milton Keynes: Paternoster, 2005), pp. 109–10.

115 This was the case in the Church of Sweden until 1996, due to the fact that the majority of the Swedish population belongs to the (Lutheran) Church of Sweden, and all children of church members were automatically enrolled as members themselves. This was in contrast to the Church of Norway, which has no unbaptized members, but has a category of people who are 'within the bounds of the Church'. The 1992 General Synod of the Church of Sweden worked to remedy the situation by finding a means for people to belong to the church whilst being on the way to baptism. From 1 January 1996 baptism became the regular requirement for membership of the Church of Sweden, but people may belong to the church on their way to baptism, and the local parish manages this through a form of regulated catechumenate. Through baptism, one is then incorporated into the church. See Ragnar Persenius, 'Baptism and Membership in the Church of Sweden', in Root and Saarinen, *op. cit.* pp. 183–95. In some countries where Christians form a small cultural minority, and baptism has come to be seen as a repudiation of one's socio-cultural heritage, people have become active members of churches whilst not wishing to be baptized. For a discussion of this situation in India, see J. Jyakiran Sebastian, 'Baptism and the Unity of the Church in India Today', in Root and Saarinen, *op. cit.* pp. 196–207.

116 Heim, *op. cit.*, pp. 150–63.

117 *Summa theologiae*, III, Q. 62, a. 6, obj. 3; also Q. 63, a. 6, *responsio*.

because it 'contains Christ substantially'.[118] Baptism is the 'start of a journey of faith, which involves turning away from the darkness of self-centredness, turning towards Christ and becoming a member of the local and worldwide Christian family'.[119] It is the seed which is sown, and which may or may not be nurtured.[120]

Whilst all churches agree that baptism is our entry into Christ, they disagree over how comprehensive baptism is: 'Some churches consider that Christian initiation is not complete without the sealing of the baptized with the gift of the Holy Spirit and participation in holy communion' (BEM n. 20). 'All agree that Christian baptism is in water and the Holy Spirit' (BEM n. 14). But 'Christians differ in their understanding as to where the sign of the gift of the Spirit is to be found . . . For some it is the water rite itself. For others, it is the anointing with chrism and/or the imposition of hands, which many churches call confirmation. For still others it is all three, as they see the Spirit operative throughout the rite' (BEM n. 14).

The issue at hand is whether one is fully initiated into Christ at baptism, or whether initiation is a fuller process. Anglicans have debated in recent decades whether baptism is complete sacramental initiation.[121] This position not only implies a non-sacramental view of confirmation, but also regards incorporation into the Body of Christ as complete regardless of participation at the Eucharist. The more usual Anglican position is that baptism is not complete initiation, but 'is the foundation sacrament of Christian initiation, which also includes catechesis, liturgical profession of faith and the confirmation of the Holy Spirit with the laying on of hands by the bishop, participation in the Eucharist and reception of Holy Communion'.[122] Christian initiation is understood as a process, culminating in that to which baptism points; reception of the bread and wine as the body and blood of Christ.

The irony in our terminology is that we use 'initiation' to mean something broader than membership itself, rather than, as might be expected, the initial rite of entry. Whilst affirming that (water) baptism renders one a member of the Body of Christ (in so far as it incorporates), we say that it does not render one fully initiated.

118 III, Q. 65, a. 3, *responsio.*

119 www.cofe.anglican.org/lifeevents/baptismconfirm/baptism1.html

120 Cf. Bryant, *op. cit.*, p. 79.

121 E. C. Whitaker, *Sacramental initiation complete in Baptism* (Bramcote: Grove liturgical study, no. 1, 1975).

122 Avis, *op. cit.*, pp. 112–13, point 6.

Water and Spirit

As noted in BEM, all agree that Christian baptism is in water and the Spirit, but churches disagree over where the sign of the gift of the Spirit is found: in the water rite itself, or a subsequent sacramental act.

New Testament witness

Paul spoke of baptism in the Spirit (I Cor. 12.13, cf. II Cor. 1.22) alongside his talk of baptism into Christ Jesus (Rom. 6.3; Gal. 3.27). In John's Gospel, Jesus teaches that one must be born of water and Spirit to enter the Kingdom of God (3.5, cf. 4.14, 7.8). It is sometimes assumed that these words point to two distinct baptisms; that water baptism is insufficient and must be followed by a separate baptism in the Spirit. However, the implication of this passage may in fact be that to be born of water is to be born of the Spirit.[123] Arguably this way of thinking has been formative in the West, even while a theology of confirmation has developed there (see below).

NT witness seems to be that the gift of the Spirit is decisive in marking one as a Christian: 'anyone who does not have the Spirit of Christ does not belong to him' (Rom. 8.9).[124] In Acts there are varying accounts of the relationship between water baptism and the gift of the Spirit. Peter calls on his audience to repent and be baptized, and they will receive the gift of the Holy Spirit (Acts 2.38). This is the sequence for the Ephesians at Acts 19.5–6. Cornelius, however, received the Spirit first, and was then baptized (10.44–8). At Pentecost (2.4) and in the case of Apollos (18.25), there is no connection between reception of the Spirit and water baptism. Arguably, the author of Acts regarded the gift of the Spirit as the most critical criterion of Christian identity, and at least did not regard water baptism as sufficient:

> Now when the apostles at Jerusalem heard that Samaria had accepted the word of God, they sent Peter and John to them. The two went down and prayed for them that they might receive the Holy Spirit (for as yet the Spirit had not come upon any of them; they had only been baptized in the name of the Lord Jesus). Then Peter and John laid their hands on them, and they received the Holy Spirit. (Acts 8.14–17)

Apollos in ch. 18 was not deemed to need rebaptizing, although he 'knew only

---

123 See Colwell, *op. cit.*, p. 113.

124 J. D. G. Dunn, especially emphasizes this view, see 'Baptism and the Unity of the Church in the New Testament', in Root and Saarinen, *op. cit.*, esp. pp. 82–5.

the baptism of John' (v. 25), presumably because his burning enthusiasm and powerful speech were signs that he had already received the Spirit.

Equally significant, however, is the fact that the early Church did not dispense with water baptism. Indeed, scholars disagree over whether the initiation rite of the apostolic church consisted originally only of water baptism, though it is likely that there were rites containing preparation, dipping in water and possibly anointing and/or the laying on of hands (cf. Acts 19.5–6).[125] Reference is made in 1 John to the *chrisma*, the anointing from the Holy One (1 John 2.20, 27), and in the Epistle to the Hebrews to the laying on of hands (Heb. 6.2). In any appeal to New Testament we should not presume that Scripture speaks plainly or with one voice; or that only the formulations and practices attested to in the NT are validated therein; or that Scripture does not need interpreting through the lenses of church traditions.[126] We can nonetheless surmise that the apostolic church did not regard the water rite alone as carrying the full weight of Christian initiation. Imposing a rich sacramental theology upon the water rite is therefore not unproblematic.[127]

The witness of the Church in the second and third centuries

It is unclear whether anointing or the imposition of hands were part of the second-century initiation rites for which we have evidence from the *Didache* and Justin. Justin's account is problematic in failing to mention the gift of the Spirit at initiation, though his silence is inconclusive. His purpose in writing was apologetic, to stress the harmlessness of Christian rites, rather than to set out a comprehensive rite.[128] In Justin's account, baptism leads directly into the Eucharist, making explicit that since baptism means entry into the Body of Christ, it conveys the right to participate in the Eucharist. The rites of initiation indicated by Hippolytus and Tertullian in the third century were practised as a unity, moving from catechumenate and immediate preparation for baptism, the threefold baptismal dipping, to anointing, laying on of hands, signing with the cross (which occurs before the laying on of hands in Tertullian *de Res.*

---

125 For example G. Beasley-Murray, *Baptism in the New Testament* (London: Macmillan, 1962); J. D. G. Dunn, *Baptism in the Holy Spirit* (London: SCM Press, 1970); A. Kavanagh, *The Shape of Baptism* (New York: Pueblo, 1978); G. W. H. Lampe, *The Seal of the Spirit*, 2nd edn (London: SPCK, 1967).

126 Dunn, 'Baptism and the Unity of the Church in the New Testament', p. 78.

127 Dunn interprets such a move as an attempt to control that which will not be controlled: the freedom of the Spirit, *ibid.*, p. 78.

128 K. W. Noakes, 'Initiation – From the New Testament Times until Cyprian', in C. Jones *et al.* (eds), *Study of the Liturgy* (London: SPCK; New York: OUP 1992), pp. 118–20.

Carn., 8), to the Paschal Eucharist. Tertullian emphasizes the Spirit's activity throughout; baptism in water by the operation of the Holy Spirit gives cleansing and remission of sins, while the ensuing laying on of hands imparts the gift of the Spirit.[129] Membership in Christ, the anointed one, was held to be conferred at the post-baptismal anointing.[130] Similarly, Cyprian speaks of baptism in water as conferring remission of sins, effecting renewal of spiritual birth and as preparing a temple ready for the Holy Spirit, whilst the Spirit is conferred at the laying on of hands, which follows immediately afterwards.[131]

Baptism in relation to confirmation and communion

Within the integrated rites of the early Church, we see the elements that would become 'confirmation' in the West – the anointing, laying on of hands and signing with cross – along with support for a theology that locates the conferring of the gift of the Spirit in the confirmation rite. We also see the basis of Eastern practice, where baptism and chrismation have remained to this day integrated into a single rite, even for infants; baptism being regarded as 'paschal' and chrismation as 'pentecostal'.[132] In Orthodox understanding, baptism restores people to their true nature by freeing them from sin and reconciling them to God and God's creation. Chrismation then takes them beyond baptism and beyond Salvation, by making them christs in Christ. Chrismation is the anointing with the Anointment of the Anointed One, and opens the door of *theosis* or deificiation. The Spirit is believed to be operative in both rites: at baptism, purifying our nature and uniting it to Christ; at chrismation, bestowing deity, the energy of the Holy Trinity which is divine grace, upon human persons.[133] East and West can agree

129 *De. Bapt.*, Chs 3, 4, 6, 8; *de Res. Carn.*, 8.

130 *De. Bapt.*, 7, *Ap. Trad.*, 21.19.

131 *Ep.*, 69.11, 73. 6, 74.5 and 7.

132 Alexander Schmemann, *The World as Sacrament* (London: Darton Longman and Todd, 1965), p. 92. Though there is no provision in modern Orthodox books for the celebration of the eucharistic liturgy as an integral part of the baptismal rite, and this is the most marked change from the rite given in the Barberini *Euchologion*, which contains the oldest surviving liturgical documents of the Byzantine rite, probably dating from late eighth or early ninth centuries. W. Jardine Grisbrooke, 'The Byzantine Rite', in Jones *et al.*, *op.cit.*, pp. 152–4; Alexander Schmemann, *Of Water and the Spirit* (Crestwood, NY: St Vladimir's Seminary Press, 1974) p. 80. The rite of baptism found in codex Barberine is in many respects similar to that described by John Chrysostom. See E. C. Whitaker, *Documents of the Baptismal Liturgy* (London: SPCK, 1970), p. 69.

133 See Merja Merras, 'Baptismal Recognition and the Orthodox Churches', in Root and Saarinen, *op. cit.*, p. 142.

significantly on the role of the Spirit across such an initiatory process. The Cyprus Agreed Statement of the International Commission for Anglican–Orthodox Theological Dialogue, *The Church of the Triune God*, 2006, states: 'At our baptism the Spirit forms Christ in us, and enables us to share in Jesus' crucifixion and resurrection. Then we begin to live in the Spirit, not primarily because extraordinary gifts instantly manifest themselves, but because the liberation of our humanity for life among God's people, accomplished in Jesus' death and resurrection, becomes a reality in us' (sect II, n. 40).

In the West, confirmation became the rite for the increasing (or sometimes it has been said the imparting) of the Holy Spirit. Increasingly it came to be practised separately from baptism, and was understood sacramentally to complete, seal or consummate baptism. Liturgically, 'to confirm' originally meant to 'make fast or sure' or to perfect or complete (*consummatio*) baptism, and did not have the association it later gained with the renewal of baptismal vows. Initial usage of the noun *confirmatio* as a liturgical term is attributed to Faustus of Riez, in a famous Whitsunday sermon around the year 460.[134] In the preceding decades the canons of the Council of Riez spoke of confirming neophytes. In this part of Gaul, there was an interval between baptism, administered by a presbyter, and the ceremony for the conferring of the Holy Spirit, which could be performed only by a bishop. When this ceremony came to be separated from the rite of baptism, it began to acquire the name 'confirmation'.

The rite of confirmation raises the question: if baptism is complete in itself, how is subsequent completion possible or necessary? Faustus addressed this question in his sermon, which is the first known attempt to provide a theology of initiation across a disintegrated rite. He said that as regards innocence, baptism is complete, and suffices for those who die forthwith, but as regards grace, in confirmation there is an increase and confirmation is necessary for those who live to face the struggles of the world; in baptism we are reborn to new life, after baptism we are confirmed for combat; in baptism we are washed, after baptism we are strengthened. He equated the gift conveyed by confirmation with the gift of the Spirit initially outpoured at Pentecost.[135] This teaching became the standard doctrine in the West in the Middle Ages on the

134 See J. D. C. Fisher and E. J. Yarnold SJ, 'The West from about AD 500 to the Reformation', in C. Jones *et al.*, *op. cit.*, pp. 149–50. Note, G. Winkler questions this attribution to Faustus, and the dating of the sermon to the mid fifth century, 'Chrismation or Confirmation? A Study in Comparative Liturgy', *Worship* 58 (1984), pp. 2–17.

135 Fisher and Yarnold SJ, *op. cit.*, pp. 149–50.

relation of baptism to confirmation,[136] there remaining, nonetheless, varying emphases over whether confirmation confers the gift of the Spirit, or completes that gift given at baptism. Aquinas, for example, regarded baptism as the sacrament of regeneration through which we receive the life of the Spirit, and confirmation as the sacrament of maturity, of the 'fulness of grace', marking the 'perfect age' of the spiritual life.[137] That the gift of the Spirit is conferred at water baptism, and furthered or completed at a later stage, is reflected in the Book of Common Prayer rites of baptism and confirmation (see below).

As the theology of confirmation developed, it became standard practice to baptize children in infancy and withhold confirmation, and/or first communion, until the child was at least seven years old. English practice insisted that a child be confirmed before being admitted to communion, in order to ensure that parents took the trouble of getting their children confirmed.[138] Baptism was typically performed by a presbyter, and confirmation was conferred by the bishop.

Initiation was spread across the years like this because of the conviction that, in order to experience all that the New Testament understands by baptism, children who were baptized as infants must make a personal confession of faith once old enough to do so. However, when confirmation is linked with the renewal of baptismal vows, and this confessional aspect is made the necessary precursor to receiving communion, confirmation comes to seem less initiatory and more about growing into Christian adulthood. The sacramental understanding of confirmation is then overshadowed.

At the Reformation, its sacramental status was questioned. Luther rejected the mediaeval rite of confirmation as a human invention, not divinely appointed, and therefore neither a sacrament nor a means of grace; to say that it conferred the Holy Spirit detracted from baptism. Similarly, Calvin denied that confirmation was a sacrament and regarded the practice of it as 'cutting off from baptism the promises proper to baptism'.[139] He sought to undo the theology that had developed since the sermon of Faustus 1,000 years before:

136 Being quoted by the author of *False Decretals*, it was read by leading authorities including Aquinas, and also Gratian, whose *Decretum* became the standard textbook of canon law for students throughout Europe.

137 *ST* III 72.1.

138 Fisher and Yarnold SJ, 'The West from about AD 500 to the Reformation', in Jones, *et al., op. cit.*, p. 151.

139 *Institutes* IV, xix, 8.

These anointers say that the Holy Spirit is given in baptism for innocence; in confirmation, for the increase of grace; that in baptism we are regenerated into life; in confirmation we are equipped for battle. And they are so shameless as to deny that baptism can be duly completed without confirmation! What wickedness! Have not we then been buried in baptism with Christ, made partakers in his death, that we may also be sharers in his resurrection [Rom. 6.4–5]? Moreover, this fellowship with Christ's death and life Paul explains to be the mortifying of our flesh and the quickening of the Spirit, because 'our old man has been crucified' [Rom. 6.6, Vg.]. In order that 'we may walk in newness of life' [Rom. 6.5, Vg.]. What is it to be equipped for battle, but this?[140]

Neither Luther nor Calvin sought a further sacramental act prior to participation in the Eucharist, but they did seek evidence of the appropriation of Christian teaching. Luther issued a shorter and a longer catechism to be learnt by children before being admitted to communion. Calvin seems not to have formalized a requirement, although Knox, while in Geneva, who also dispensed with a rite of confirmation, admitted children to communion once they could say the Lord's Prayer, Creed and Ten Commandments.

The Book of Common Prayer reflects the Reformers' concerns over personal understanding and confession of the faith, though it takes a modified stance influenced by Erasmus. Erasmus recommended that profession of faith be renewed in public ceremonies performed by bishops, ceremonies which may have included an Episcopal laying on of hands.[141] The 1549 Prayer Book contains an order 'of confirmation or laying on of hands upon those that are baptized and come to years of discretion'. The rite is to be administered only to those who can say in their mother tongue the Creed, Lord's Prayer and the Ten Commandments, and can answer questions from the catechism put to them by the bishop. This put an end to the confirmation of infants, which, although rare in the later Middle Ages, was still permissible as late as 1533 when Princess Elizabeth was baptized and confirmed at three days old. In the Prayer Book of 1662, the catechism is separated from the order of confirmation. The bishop asks candidates to 'renew the solemn promise and vow that was made in your name at your baptism, ratifying and confirming the same in your own persons'. The gift of the Holy Spirit is believed to be conferred at baptism; the priest praying,

---

140 *Institutes* IV, xix, 8.
141 J. D. C. Fisher, 'Lutheran, Anglican and Reformed Rites', in Jones *et al.*, *op. cit.*, p. 162.

> Give thy holy Spirit to *these persons*; that, being now born again and
> made *heirs* of everlasting salvation, through our Lord Jesus Christ, *they*
> may continue thy *servants*, and attain thy promises.[142]

At confirmation, the bishop lays hands on the candidate, with the words:

> Defend, O Lord, this thy Child with thy heavenly grace, that *he* may
> continue thine for ever; and daily increase in thy holy Spirit more and
> more, until *he* come unto thy everlasting kingdom.[143]

Re-integrated rites

Initiation may happen over time or in a single rite. Either way, it is a process
of which baptism is the foundation sacrament, and throughout which the
Spirit is operative. The Alternative Service Book (1980) reintegrated the
stages of initiation with a single rite of 'Baptism, Confirmation, and Holy
Communion'. *Common Worship* has retained the option of a single rite,
'Baptism and Confirmation at the Order for Celebration of Holy
Communion'.

Even where the three landmarks of initiation are integrated into a single rite,
there are aspects of the process of initiation which precede and proceed the
rite. Some such ways have been formalized by the Roman Catholic Church in
the USA, in the Rite of the Christian Initiation of Adults (RCIA), which has
influenced the Church of England *Rites on the Way*. RCIA sets out a number of
stages of welcome, teaching, enrolment, and continuing conversion which
happen over several weeks. These stages are punctuated by liturgical rites, and
lead toward the final rite, usually at the Easter Vigil, where candidates are
baptized, confirmed, anointed with oil, and where they receive communion.
They thereby become full members of the Roman Catholic Church. This final
rite is followed by a fifty-day period of mystagogy, reflecting on the paschal
mystery, the conclusion of which marks the end of the initiation process. This
moves the time of full initiation even beyond participation in the Eucharist,
and, as we noted in respect of Anglican terminology, contains the irony that
'full initiation' entails something broader than 'full membership'. The World
Council of Churches Faith and Order text-in-progress, 'One Baptism: Towards
Mutual Recognition' (2006), goes several steps further in declaring that

142 *Book of Common Prayer* (Oxford University Press), p. 248.

143 *Ibid.*, p. 360. Similarly Bucer, also influenced by Erasmus, seem to have believed that
children received the Holy Spirit at baptism but received an increase of the Spirit at
confirmation. See Fisher, *op. cit.*, pp. 162–3.

'Christian initiation is a process which is not completed this side of the Kingdom' (n. 7). This statement would seem to make more sense with respect to 'salvation' or 'theosis/deification' than it does with respect to 'initiation', unless by 'initiation' we mean a process that we do not get beyond: our beginnings which we always carry with us.

It is true of our baptism that we never surpass it, and are continually invited to reappropriate it. 'One Baptism: Towards Mutual Recognition' conveys that baptism has an eschatological dimension, looking forward to the fullness of time.[144] What is promised in baptism is none other than the Kingdom of God. The Kingdom may not be fully realized in this age. Nonetheless, the Kingdom breaks into our present time, and we can be more or less open to it doing so.[145]

The awkwardness of the term 'initiation' for conveying the development or the fullness of our life in Christ comes even more sharply into view within such eschatologically orientated statements. The notion of initiation carries with it a sense that at some point you move beyond the stage of initiation, whereas we never move beyond our appropriation of the death and resurrection of Christ. We constantly re-enter that death and resurrection.

Complete but continual

There is a continual element not only in the process of initiation but in baptism itself. While baptism does not need to be repeated or (*qua* baptism) completed,[146] it is yet to be fulfilled.[147] Fulfilment does come immediately for two reasons, at least: 1. we fall back into our old, slave-like ways, which is the problem of post-baptismal sin; and 2. our transformation is a process and takes time.

1. Post-baptismal sin

In baptism we die with Christ and are raised in him to new life, but we do not automatically remove ourselves from the slave culture. We still live with a spirit

144 Faith and Order Paper No. 111, published 1982. On this eschatological dimension, and baptism as a call to struggle against the forces of wickedness, see The Cyprus Agreed Statement, *The Church of the Triune God*, section IV, n. 17.

145 S. K. Wood, *One Baptism: Ecumenical Dimensions of the Doctrine of Baptism* (Collegeville, MN: Liturgical Press, 2009): ch. 1, explores the ways in which baptism is 'inaugurated eschatology, the end time present now', p. 1.

146 Avis, *op. cit.*, p. 14.

147 Cf. Schmemann, *op. cit.*

of slavery, not realizing that we have been made children of God (Rom. 8.15), or that in being made God's children we live in a new kingdom with a new set of values. We claim to have fellowship with God whilst walking in darkness (1 John 1.6).

The question of post-baptismal sin is whether we thereby lose what our baptism has bestowed. The answer is no. God has a way of maintaining the relationship. This way does not require re-baptism. It involves confession and points us towards the Eucharist.

By confessing our sins we open ourselves up to God's forgiveness: 'If we say that we have no sin, we deceive ourselves, and the truth is not in us. If we confess our sins, he who is faithful and just will forgive us our sins and cleanse us from all unrighteousness' (1 John 1.8–9). Baptism itself is the type by which we best understand confession, for each time we confess we die a bit more, and ask that we might be granted to serve God 'in newness of life'. And the Eucharist consummates God's forgiveness, for it is through Christ's atoning sacrifice that we are forgiven, and the Eucharist extends and mediates that sacrifice through time: 'My little children, I am writing these things to you so that you may not sin. But if anyone does sin, we have an advocate with the Father, Jesus Christ the righteous; and he is the atoning sacrifice for our sins, and not for ours only but also for the sins of the whole world' (1 John 2.1–2). The Eucharist puts us in touch with the once-for-all paschal event. It makes sacramentally present and communicates the act that remits sins. For this reason, 'the forgiveness which makes the Christian fit to receive the Lord's supper *truly* is directly produced by the memorial itself'.[148]

The Eucharistic community, if it has understood all this, is made up of those who know themselves to be all too prone to slip back into sin, who dare to be honest about that, and who know that although we are sinners we can still walk with God (whereas not to know oneself as forgiven by God is not to know this).[149] Our time in the waters of baptism as both our tomb and mother, need not happen again. Yet, in our relationship with God and one another, we must continually die and be reborn, making our passage out of the world of sin and debt until we are fully transformed into the likeness of Christ.

> Grant, Lord, that we who are baptized into the death of your Son

---

148 J.-M. Tillard, 'The Bread and Cup of Reconciliation', in E. Schillebeekcx (ed.), *The Sacramental Administration of Reconciliation* (*Concilium* I.7) (London: Burns & Oates, 1971), pp. 47, 50.

149 D. Z. Phillips, *The Concept of Prayer* (New York: Schocken Books, 1966), pp. 67–8.

our Saviour Jesus Christ may continually put to death our evil desires and be buried with him; and that through the grave and gate of death we may pass to our joyful resurrection; through his merits who died and was buried and rose again for us, your Son Jesus Christ our Lord.[150]

Dying to ourselves, displacing ourselves from the centre, is living out our baptism. We cannot do more than that; we cannot move onto another stage where something different is required. The invitation is always to go back and die again. Because of this, the anthropological notion of initiation is misleading: we are not moving onwards and upwards to new challenges and spiritual activities. We have ever before us the same challenge and spiritual demand, to die with Christ and pass into the resurrection life.

2. Transformation

That our transformation does not happen instantaneously is an act of mercy, for otherwise we would not recognize ourselves in our changed nature, nor would we exercise freedom and responsibility with respect to the ways in which we are changed. Baptism brings us into a life of new values, and by giving ourselves to this new life and its values, we are shaped by them. We are free to withhold ourselves, and free to give more and more of ourselves. 'Baptism is related not only to momentary experience, but to life-long growth into Christ' (BEM para 9), and, indeed, beyond, in that baptism has an eschatological dimension, looking forward to the fullness of time.[151] Prayer mediates this transformation. Gregory of Sinai had called prayer 'the manifestation of baptism' because in baptism Christ and the Holy Spirit come to dwell in our hearts.[152] Herbert McCabe OP describes all our prayer '[as] an abandonment of ourselves . . . because it is a sharing in Christ's abandonment of himself in death':

> In prayer we stop believing in ourselves, relying on ourselves, and we believe and trust in God. It is all a sharing in Christ's death . . . looking

---

150 Collect, Evening Prayer on Friday, *Common Worship Daily Prayer* (London: Church House Publishing, 2005), p. 190.

151 On this eschatological dimension, and baptism as a call to struggle against the forces of wickedness, see The Cyprus Agreed Statement, *The Church of the Triune God*, Sect IV, n. 17.

152 'The Signs of Grace and Delusion'. See S. Tugwell OP, 'The Manifestation of Baptism', *New Blackfriars*, 52/614 (1971), pp. 324–30; S. Tugwell OP, 'Reflections on the Pentecostal Doctrine of "Baptism in the Holy Spirit" II', *Heythrop Journal*, 13/4 (1972), pp. 402–14.

forward to that ultimate sharing in his death which is our own death in him, through which we rise in him to understand the Father in the Son, to pray the prayer which is the Spirit, to communicate with our Father in joy and love for eternity.[153]

All our prayer is a sharing in the eternal exchange between the Father and Son, the Son casting himself upon the Father, and the Father raising him up. Hence, the Eucharist, the sacrament of the death and resurrection of Christ, is our central prayer.[154] So BEM speaks of the Eucharist constantly reaffirming baptism (BEM, Commentary 14 (c)), and subsequent Faith and Order work on baptismal unity clarifies that the 'way of discipleship is marked daily by the baptismal experience of dying to self and sin and rising with Christ to forgiveness and new life, experiences which are focussed sacramentally in the eucharist'.[155]

Sadly, however, while churches are agreed that baptism incorporates us into Christ, they are not united, and our Eucharistic unity proves harder to realize than our baptismal unity. We cannot rely on baptism alone as a basis for unity, because the Eucharist itself is instrumental in sustaining us as members of the Body of Christ. Just as baptism which was not orientated towards the Eucharist would be deficient, so baptismal unity which is not orientated towards Eucharistic unity is lacking.

The ecumenical theology of mutual recognition of baptism

That is not to say, however, that ecumenical relations cannot be greatly enhanced by focusing on our baptism in Christ. In the processes leading up to BEM, and since its publication, ecumenists have worked on the potential of baptism to bring the churches together.[156] The different churches are agreed

153 H. McCabe OP, *God Still Matters* (London: Continuum, 2002), p. 218.

154 *Ibid.*, p. 217.

155 'One Baptism, Towards Mutual Recognition', a text in progress, World Council of Churches Faith and Order Commission, 2006, n. 35.

156 For an overview see A. Birmelé, 'Baptism and the Unity of the Church in Ecumenical Dialogues', in Root and Saarinen, *op. cit.*, pp. 104–29. For on-going endeavour, see 'One Baptism, Towards Mutual Recognition', a text in progress, World Council of Churches Faith and Order Commission, 2006. The churches' responses to BEM are published in six volumes: M. Thurian (ed.) *Churches Respond to BEM*, Faith and Order Papers, Nos. 129, 132, 135, 137, 143, 144 (Geneva: WCC, 1986–88). On Anglican endeavours before and after BEM, see Colin Davey, 'The Ecclesial Significance of Baptism According to Anglican Ecumenical Documents', *One in Christ*, Vol. XXXV, 1999, No. 2, p. 133.

that baptism incorporates us into Christ; that there is only one baptism, with Christ the agent of it (cf. I Cor. 1); and that since baptism points towards participation in the sacrament of the body and blood of Christ, our baptismal unity has a bearing on our Eucharistic unity. 'Through baptism, Christians are brought into union with Christ, with each other and with the Church of every time and place. Our common baptism, which unites us to Christ in faith, is thus a basic bond of unity' (BEM n. 6, commentary).

BEM summed up the ecumenical potential, responsibility and hope contained in our baptism:

> We are one people and are called to confess and serve one Lord in each place and in all the world. The union with Christ which we share through baptism has important implications for Christian unity. 'There is . . . one baptism, one God and Father of us all . . . ' (Eph. 4.4—6). When baptismal unity is realized in one holy, catholic, apostolic Church, a genuine Christian witness can be made to the healing and reconciling love of God. Therefore, our one baptism into Christ constitutes a call to the churches to overcome their divisions and visibly manifest their fellowship. (BEM n. 6, commentary)

At present, however, churches are unable 'mutually to recognize their various practices of baptism as sharing in the one baptism', or are actually divided 'in spite of mutual baptismal recognition' (BEM n. 6, commentary).

BEM n. 6 identifies two sets of problems or scenarios:

1. the failure of churches to recognize one another's practices of baptism as sharing in the one baptism, i.e., where mutual recognition of baptism is lacking;

2. where there is mutual recognition of baptism, but churches still remain divided.

There is a third scenario in ecumenical relations:

3: where baptismal unity is accompanied by Eucharistic unity, and sometimes also by mutual recognition of one another's ministries.

Below we will consider instances of each of these scenarios. Before we do that, we need to be aware that although BEM placed the 'need to recover baptismal unity . . . at the heart of the ecumenical task' (n. 6, commentary), the WCC has put on hold (until 2013) further exploration of One Baptism Towards Mutual Recognition. There is some wariness about baptism being used as a

Trojan horse. As we will see below, the Orthodox, by a process of economy, acknowledge that something called baptism has happened in our churches. If they were to be pushed further on this, the delicate arrangement that currently works might come apart, for they would find it difficult to validate baptisms that are performed without chrismation, or to accept that Western baptisms are the same as Eastern baptisms. Recognizing baptism in other communities implies recognizing authorized ministers in those communities, which implies acknowledging that those communities are, in (almost) all ecumenically significant respects, true churches, or churches 'like ours'. Different communities have managed to travel varying distances with one another in these respects.

1. Where mutual recognition of baptism is lacking

For Baptists, as heirs of the Radical Reformation, problems of mutual baptismal recognition arise because they do not agree with other communions that baptism is the foundation of the Church. They do not see baptism as necessary either for salvation or for membership of the Church.

Like the Orthodox, who also struggle with the mutual recognition of baptism, Baptists worry that other churches have misunderstood and failed to imitate the baptism of the early Church. Unlike the Orthodox, they see believer's baptism by immersion as the only clear New Testament practice. Baptists recognize Christians by their personal confession of faith. They do not recognize as baptism a water rite practised on someone incapable of personal confession of faith. Nonetheless, they commonly recognize the baptisms of those baptized as believers, but not by immersion, in other communions. Therefore, ironically, Baptists are able to recognize as Christians and as parts of the one Church, a 'congregation made up of persons all baptized as infants. . .who individually confess their belief in Christ'.[157]

Baptists question the direction of ecumenical debate, when it moves from baptism to the nature of the Church. They do not regard mutual recognition of the baptism of individuals as the first or 'easiest' step in ecumenical endeavour, nor do they think we can proceed from there to 'more difficult' matters of recognizing ecclesial realities such as ministry and sacrament.[158] Instead they move from the nature of the Church to the meaning of baptism:

157 Heim, *op. cit.*, pp. 151–2.

158 'Believing and Being Baptized: Baptism, So-Called Re-baptism and Children in Church', a discussion document by the Doctrine and Worship Committee of the Baptist Union of Great Britain, 1996, pp. 22–3, quoted by Heim, *op. cit.*, p. 152.

> it is because we understand the core of the church community to be committed disciples of Christ. . .that we understand baptism to be the seal of the Spirit for a believing and obedient disciple. At the same time, this means that we can recognize the realities of church and ministry existing among others, regardless of the mode of baptism they exercise.[159]

Therefore, it is not so much qualms over infant baptism that prevent Baptists from recognizing the baptisms of other churches. It is the ecclesiology of the gathered church, and the ability of congregations to be self-regulating: 'If recognition of other churches' baptisms requires Baptists to relinquish the capacity to regulate their own membership so as to constitute their congregations as communities of professed believers, then this recognition will not be forthcoming'.[160] These concerns might be met by introducing ideas of gradation of membership, where non-Baptist churches have a catechumenate linked to confirmation of one's infant baptism. This would help to overcome the ambiguities in our terminology of 'membership', as noted above, whilst also emphasizing the similarities between churches that practice confirmation and those that hold services of reception into the community. But the bigger issue at stake is the direction of Baptist thinking, if Baptist ecclesiology moves from the nature of the Church to baptism, rather than vice versa. Baptists would then not affirm that baptism is the foundation of the Church.

Why affirm that baptism is the foundation of the Church? Because the Church and our membership of it begin and rest entirely in what Christ has done, in bringing us through death so that we are now incorporated into his new life. On this matter, the Orthodox and Anglicans have reached a significant agreed statement:

> In his own person, fully human and fully divine, Christ renews humanity disfigured by sin. In his body the Church, through the indwelling of the Holy Spirit, sinful human beings are brought, through faith and the sacraments, into communion with God, for which they were created . . .

> To reach eternal life in communion with God and each other, we must be open in humility to the gift of God's new life; we must die to the old life and be born again in the waters of baptism (John 3.3, 7). In order to

---

159 *Ibid.*
160 Heim, *op. cit.*, p. 156.

come to the table of the Lord for the eucharistic banquet of his Body and Blood we must first be baptized in the name of the Father, the Son and the Holy Spirit (Matt. 28.18–20), and so be conformed to his death and resurrection. But that is not all. The grace of God in sacramental mystery draws us to a life in the world of love for God and neighbour expressed in devotion to 'the apostles' teaching and fellowship, to the breaking of bread and the prayers' (Acts 2.42) and in charity to the poor (Acts 2.44–45; 4.32).[161]

Hope lies here for progress towards full baptismal unity. Until now, Orthodox churches have found it difficult to recognize in principle the validity of baptism outside Orthodox churches.[162] They find that 'BEM does not sufficiently note the aspect of anointing in baptism and does not clarify what is the church to which the neophyte is being joined and what is the faith he/she is to confess'.[163] They are also unhappy about the lack of the sacrament of chrismation in the document, and find it difficult to align themselves with churches that practice confirmation separately from baptism.[164] The Orthodox Church has not fully recognized the baptisms of the Roman Catholic Church and the churches of the Reformation, but it follows the principle of economy regarding them; that in theory the Orthodox Church does not recognize the baptism of these churches to be the baptism of the early Church, but in practice accepts it and therefore does not baptize those who come from these churches into the Orthodox Church.[165] The International Commission for Anglican–Orthodox theological dialogue has agreed, in the context of discussing women and men and ministries in the Church:

> The 'one baptism for the forgiveness of sins' in which Anglicans and Orthodox alike proclaim their common faith in the Niceno-Constantinopolitan creed is conferred without distinction on females and males. All the ministries of the Church, lay and ordained, presuppose the grace of this foundational sacrament of the Christian life.[166]

---

161 *The Church of the Triune God*, The Cyprus Agreed Statement of the International Commission for Anglican–Orthodox Theological Dialogue, 2006, Sect I, nn. 7 and 8.

162 For helpful explication see W. Kasper, 'Ecclesiological and Ecumenical Implications of Baptism', *Ecumenical Review*, Oct. 2000.

163 Merras, op. cit., p. 143.

164 *Ibid.*, pp. 143–4.

165 *Ibid.*, p. 144.

166 *The Church of the Triune God*, The Cyprus Agreed Statement of the International Commission for Anglican–Orthodox Theological Dialogue, 2006, Sect VII, n. 5.

2. Mutual recognition of baptism which does not yield fuller unity

However, even where baptismal unity is affirmed, it has yielded disappointingly thin results, ecclesiologically, in some contexts. The Common Certificate of Baptism was produced in 1972 by the British Council of Churches. The initial request for this arose in Scotland, in the need for documentation for mixed marriages involving the Roman Catholic Church there. The churches agreeing to use this common certificate include the four Anglican Churches in England, Scotland, Wales and Ireland, the Congregational, Lutheran, Methodist, Moravian, Presbyterian, Reformed and Roman Catholic Churches. Whilst this is of great practical benefit, it is not indicative of a rich, emergent ecumenical ecclesiology. The certificate operates as a kind of passport or identity card, rather than signifying a change in relationship between the churches themselves.[167] As the 1996 report, *Called to be One*, from the Churches Together in England, put it:

> At its lowest it means that a person baptized in one of the Churches which formally accepted the certificate would not be rebaptized if he or she sought to become a member of another Church that accepted the certificate. In itself it does not necessarily mean that person's membership of the Church will be legally or canonically recognized in the other Church.[168]

Mutual recognition of baptism is therefore only a first step towards mutual recognition of Church membership. In practice, most churches recognize one another's members as 'member[s] of Christ and of his body, the Church',[169] but do not thereby recognize them as members of their own communions, an exception being the Porvoo churches (see below).

The Faith and Order text-in-progress, 'One Baptism; Towards Mutual Recognition', notes that:

> There are at least three dimensions to mutual recognition: recognizing one another individually as Christians; churches recognizing the baptism of a person from one faith community who seeks entrance into another; and churches recognizing one another as churches, that is, as authentic expressions of the One Church of Jesus Christ.[170]

167 Davey, *op. cit.*, p. 133.

168 *Called to be One*, 1996, Appendix B: Christian Initiation and Church Membership, p. 67.

169 *Ibid.*, p. 67.

170 'One Baptism, Towards Mutual Recognition', a text in progress, World Council of Churches Faith and Order Commission, 2006, n. 10.

We have seen that the Orthodox Church in practice (even if not fully in theory) operates in the first two dimensions. The Roman Catholic Church does also. Neither Rome nor the East can endorse the third dimension. This is explicit in the stance taken at Vatican II, which spoke of those who 'believe in Christ and have been properly baptized' as being in some, though imperfect, communion with the Catholic Church:

> For men who believe in Christ and have been truly baptized are in communion with the Catholic Church even though this communion is imperfect. The differences that exist in varying degrees between them and the Catholic Church – whether in doctrine and sometimes in discipline, or concerning the structure of the Church – do indeed create many obstacles, sometimes serious ones, to full ecclesiastical communion. The ecumenical movement is striving to overcome these obstacles. But even in spite of them it remains true that all who have been justified by faith in Baptism are members of Christ's body, and have a right to be called Christian, and so are correctly accepted as brothers by the children of the Catholic Church . . .
>
> Nevertheless, our separated brethren, whether considered as individuals or as Communities and Churches, are not blessed with that unity which Jesus Christ wished to bestow on all those who through Him were born again into one body, and with Him quickened to newness of life – that unity which the Holy Scriptures and the ancient Tradition of the Church proclaim. For it is only through Christ's Catholic Church, which is 'the all-embracing means of salvation,' that they can benefit fully from the means of salvation. We believe that Our Lord entrusted all the blessings of the New Covenant to the apostolic college alone, of which Peter is the head, in order to establish the one Body of Christ on earth to which all should be fully incorporated who belong in any way to the people of God.[171]

What do we want to say about the seeming anomaly that churches can recognize believers as members of Christ's body, the universal Church, but not of their own communion due to something wanting in their doctrine, discipline or church structure? 'Has Christ been divided? Was Paul crucified for you? Or were you baptized in the name of Paul?' (1 Cor. 1.12). Do Paul's admonitions of the Christians in Corinth, when they are setting up divisions

---

171 Decree On Ecumenism, *Unitatis Redintegratio*, 3.

amongst themselves according to their different teachers and forebears in Christ, apply on the scale of church communities, or only to individuals?

For church communities to apply it to themselves, they must first recognize one another as true churches, and here is the rub. Roman Catholic difficulties with recognizing the baptism of others stems from early Church struggles over how to deal with Christians who had received baptism in a heretical or schismatic community.[172] The Roman Catholic position follows the Augustinian rather than Cyrpian line.

Cyprian of Carthage argued that since heretics and schismatics stand outside the one church, they do not possess the Spirit – and hence cannot impart it. Their 'baptism' is without effect; it is not a baptism. So, while he insisted that there is only one true church, only one Spirit and one baptism,[173] this one baptism was not possessed by heretics and schismatics since they were not in the true church. If they sought fellowship in the Catholic Church they would need not rebaptism but simply baptism.[174]

By contrast Pope Stephen I of Rome and the church of Alexandria recognized the validity of baptism outside the church. For Stephen I, the criterion was the invocation of the name of the triune God (*Ep.* 74.5, 75.9).[175] The West generally embraced this position at the synod of Arles (314).

Augustine's dispute with the Donatists became crucial for the whole further development of the West, and even for the Reformers of the sixteenth century. Augustine argued that baptism is valid outside the Catholic Church because the real bestower of baptism is Jesus Christ himself.[176] Crucially, for Augustine there are no sacraments outside the Church. Hence, even where heretics usurp the sacraments they remain the Church's sacraments. Therefore one must distinguish the heretics' doctrines from their use of the sacraments, which belong to Christ and the Church.[177] Donatists perform a valid baptism, but it does not become efficacious until brought within the order of the Church.

Thus we arrive at the position where baptism within other 'churches' can be

172 For the following account, I am grateful for W. Kasper's 'Ecclesiological and Ecumenical Implications of Baptism', *The Ecumenical Review*, Oct. 2000.

173 *Ep.* 71.1, 74.4.

174 *Ep.* 74,7.

175 For receiving heretics he required only the laying-on of hands, as an act of penance (DS 110).

176 *De bapt.* IV, 12,18; In John VI,7; *Ep.* 93, 47.

177 *De bapt.* I, 12,19. However, he did not accept that the validity of their baptism extended to its fruitfulness (*ibid.*, 6.1. I).

recognized, but not the authenticity of those 'churches'. We have a unity in potentiality. As with all that flows from our baptism, there is much that is awaiting fulfilment. The ARCIC process, however, is evidence of the progress that can be made based upon baptismal unity, and of an openness to significant advances in the future. *Elucidations on Authority in the Church, The Final Report,* 1981 declares that although our communities have been separated for 400 years, '[m]any bonds still unite us: we confess the same faith in the one true God; we have received the same Spirit; we have been baptized with the same baptism; and we preach the same Christ' (n. 1). The Report is specific that the issues dividing the communities are not baptismal, but are 'centered on the eucharist, on the meaning and function of ordained ministry, and on the nature and exercise of authority in the Church', and it is hopeful that 'substantial agreement on these divisive issues is now possible (n. 2).The ARCIC Report, *Church as Communion* (1991), acknowledges that our two churches 'share in the communion founded upon the saving life and work of Christ and his continuing presence through the Holy', and emphasizes 'our common baptism into Christ' (quoting the Common Declaration of John Paul II and Archbishop Robert Runcie of 2 October 1989) (*Church as Communion* n. 50). It also notes a sharing of gifts in spirituality and worship, and a 'notable convergence in our patterns of liturgy, especially in that of the eucharist' (n. 51). These forms of sharing are accepted as shaping the on-going approaches to unresolved matters which are the 'effects of our centuries of separation', and which have led to 'divergent patterns of authority' and differences in 'perceptions and practices' (nn. 57, 53).

3. Beyond mutual recognition of baptism towards fuller unity

Even without formal recognition of ministries, Anglican churches have found that on the basis of baptism they can admit members of other churches to full participation in the Eucharist. In 1972, the Church of England passed Canon B15A (b) which declared: 'There shall be admitted to Holy Communion . . . baptized persons who are communicant members of other Churches which subscribe to the doctrine of the Holy Trinity, and who are in good standing in their own Church.' This followed on from the recommendations of the Lambeth Conference of 1968, that:

> in order to meet special pastoral needs of God's people, under the direction of the bishop Christians duly baptized in the name of the Holy Trinity and qualified to receive Holy Communion in their own Churches

> may be welcomed at the Lord's Table in the Anglican Communion.
> (Lambeth Conference 1968, Resolution 45)

And that:

> Anglican communicants be free to attend the Eucharist in other
> Churches holding the apostolic faith as contained in the Scriptures and
> summarized in the Apostles' and Nicene Creeds, and as conscience
> dictates to receive the sacrament, when they know they are welcome to
> do so. (Resolution 46)

This level of unity can be furthered by mutual recognition of one another's
ordained ministries and Episcopal office. For example, BEM led the Church in
Wales to re-evaluate its practice of insisting upon 'episcopal confirmation
before admitting members of other churches to full membership'.[178]

The Porvoo churches have most fully worked through the ecumenical
significance of baptism. These churches 'acknowledge that in all our Churches
the Word of God is authentically preached, and the sacraments of baptism and
the Eucharist are duly administered'. They 'welcome one another's members
to receive sacramental and other pastoral ministrations', and 'regard baptized
members of all our Churches as members of our own'. Here, mutual
recognition of baptism reaches its highest expression: baptized persons are
recognized as members of the Universal Church and therefore of one another's
communions.

Dying to self, ecumenically

Where Paul taught the Christians in Corinth to recognize their need of one
another (1 Cor. 12), this also applies on the larger scale concerning the
relationship between churches. Ecumenically, churches are mindful of 1
Corinthians 12. They do acknowledge what they learn from one another, and
the gifts that each contributes. Can we also apply on a larger scale Paul's
chastisement of those same Christians, for setting up divisions amongst
themselves because of the different teachers they followed (1 Cor. 1)? Paul
reminds them that they have all been baptized in Christ and that Christ is not
divided.

Our baptism means that we are brothers and sisters to one another through
Christ, and only through Christ. As individuals, our way to one another is

---

178 *Churches Respond to BEM*, Vol. III, 1987, p. 82; Davey, *op. cit.*, p. 135.

frequently blocked by our egos, as Bonhoeffer puts it in *Life Together*.[179] No doubt this is also true of us on the larger scale, as distinct church communities. Ecumenism works, partly, by churches asking what gifts they can bring to teach one other, and how they can be responsible in helping one another to fulfil or live worthily of their baptism. It also involves distinct communities seeking to work out and retain their integrity. But, these communities also need to live baptismally: to die, or practice self-abandonment, in that way of making room for Christ and for one another. A difficulty in acknowledging this is that Paul spoke of dying to sin (Rom. 6), and churches are hard-pressed to regard themselves as sinners, when bringing their wisdom and traditions to the ecumenical table. Yet, where sin is understood as the prioritizing of some goods over the one really important thing,[180] ecumenically the challenge to die to sin involves the challenge collectively to discern in each instance what the really important thing is. As churches grow in wisdom and tradition, they retain sight of their basic and shared identity in Christ by the baptismal discipline of continually dying. This is what refines them, and purifies their wisdom and traditions. As Bonhoeffer writes:

> Not what a man is in himself as a Christian, his spirituality and piety, constitutes the basis of our community. What determines our brotherhood is what that man is by reason of Christ. Our community with one another consists solely in what Christ has done to both of us. This is true not merely at the beginning, as though in the course of time something else were to be added to our community; it remains so for all the future and to all eternity. I have community with others and I shall continue to have it only through Jesus Christ. The more genuine and the deeper our community becomes, the more will everything else between us recede, the more clearly and purely will Jesus Christ and his work become the one and only thing that is vital between us. We have one another only through Christ, but through Christ we do have one another, wholly, and for all eternity.[181]

Although Bonhoeffer does not explicitly say so, this is a baptismal account of Christian community. Like slaves whose debt has been cancelled because of what their king has done, Christians are related to one another by what Christ has done to them.

Bonhoeffer's account is also a Eucharistic account of a Christian community,

---

179 Bonhoeffer, *op. cit.*, p. 12.
180 Cf. H. McCabe, *God, Christ and Us* (London and New York: Continuum, 2003), p. 30.
181 Bonhoeffer, *op. cit.*, p. 14.

because what Christ has done to us, in dying and taking us with him, is made present again at each Eucharist. Our baptism foreshadows the Eucharist, and what we receive at the Eucharist is the identity that we received at our baptism.

Baptism is the start of our life together, the basis of our unity, and the foundation of the Church. It is also, ultimately, the only identity we claim. Ecumencially, we need to start with what God has done to and in us, and not with the history of our different communions and their interactions. Or rather, we tell our history not because that is a good starting point or basis for ecumenical dialogue, but because and in so far as that history reflects what God has done to and in us. We take our histories seriously because we have been baptized, and because we have been baptized we need to stay radically in touch with who we are; the radical dynamic of going back to our roots lends a purifying lens through which to view our history. As we move out from baptismal unity to fuller unity on other and all matters, we also pare ourselves back to realizing the fundamental baptismal truth, that we are who we are because we died with Christ and have been raised with and in him. In this lies our new birth, our new identity, and the basis of our relationship with one another. The 'essence of baptism and the gift of the Spirit is Christological and ecclesiological. ". . . don't you know that all of us who were baptized into Christ Jesus were baptized into his death? We were therefore buried with him through baptism into death in order that, just as Christ was raised from the dead through the glory of the Father, we too may live a new life"' (Rom. 6.3–4).[182]

---

182 Colwell, *op. cit,*, p. 120.

5

Confirmation and Christian unity

Martin Davie

Introduction

The mutual recognition of baptism among the churches underpins much ecumenical progress. What is less well known is that there is also broad agreement on confirmation. One of the points that is highlighted in the World Council of Churches statement *Baptism, Eucharist and Ministry (BEM)*, and that has been highlighted in other ecumenical texts as well, is the development of ecumenical agreement about baptism. Churches that are still divided from one another have been able to recognize common features in their understanding and practice of baptism and this has led to widespread mutual recognition of each other's baptisms. As *BEM* puts it:

> Churches are increasingly recognizing one another's baptism as the one baptism into Christ when Jesus Christ has been confessed as Lord by the candidate, or in the case of infant baptism, when confession has been made by the church (parents, guardians, godparents and congregation) and affirmed later by personal faith and commitment.[183]

What also needs to be recognized is that alongside this common understanding and practice of baptism there is also, among many Western Churches at least, a similar common understanding and practice of confirmation.

This paper begins by outlining this common understanding and practice of confirmation. It then goes on to look at the contribution that the theology and practice of confirmation might make to ecumenical dialogue with Christians in the Baptist tradition and the difference between confirmation and chrismation. Finally, it considers the place of confirmation in dialogue with those in the Pentecostal tradition and concludes by exploring three

---

183 *Baptism, Eucharist and Ministry* (Geneva: World Council of Churches, 1982), p. 6.

areas of continuing disagreement between the churches concerning confirmation.

1. A similar pattern of confirmation rites

If we compare confirmation services from the Church of England, the Latin Rite in the Roman Catholic Church,[184] the Lutheran tradition,[185] the EKD,[186] the Methodist Church,[187] the United Reformed Church[188] the Church of Scotland[189] and the Moravian Church[190] we see a strikingly similar pattern in their confirmation rites.

There are obviously differences in detail between the rites, but what is striking is the fact that all the rites contain a series of common elements occurring in much the same order:[191]

- An affirmation of baptismal promises;

- A Trinitarian profession of faith (mostly using the words of the Apostles' Creed);

- A prayer for God to strengthen the candidates through His Spirit (this is implicit in the EKD and United Reformed Church rite and in all the other rites except the Church of Scotland rite it is linked to the sevenfold gifting promised in Isa. 11);

- Some form of commitment to living the Christian life as part of the Church;

- The presiding minister laying his/her hand on the head of each candidate.[192]

184 See the sections of *The Catechism of the Catholic Church* cited below.

185 See *Evangelical Lutheran Worship* (Minneapolis: Fortress Press, 2006), pp. 234–7.

186 See for example the Confirmation rite of the Evangelische Landeskirche in Württemberg.

187 See *The Methodist Worship Book* (Peterborough: Methodist Publishing House, 1999), pp. 97–101.

188 See *Worship: from the United Reformed Church* (London: The United Reformed Church, 2003), pp. 67–72.

189 See the 'Order for the Public Profession of Faith, Confirmation and Admission to the Lord's Supper', in *The Book of Common Order of the Church of Scotland*, 2nd edn (Edinburgh: St Andrew Press, 2005).

190 See the *Anglican–Moravian Conversations* (London: CCU, 1996, p.18) and the *Church Order of the Unitas Fratrum* (Order of the Unity Synod, 1995), p. 65.

191 The only real variation is that in the URC rite the profession of faith precedes rather than follows the re-affirmation of the baptismal promises.

192 Although this is optional in the Lutheran rite provision is still made for it.

- Some form of welcome to the newly confirmed by the members of the local Christian community.[193]

Furthermore, even though different forms of words are used, there is a striking similarity in the content of the re-affirmation of the baptismal promises, the profession of faith, the prayer for the gift of the Spirit, and the words accompanying the laying of the hand on the candidate's head. In the case of the Roman Catholic rite the context makes it clear that what is meant by the words 'be sealed with the Gift of the Holy Spirit' is the same as what is meant by the prayer that God will confirm the candidate with the Spirit used in the other rites.

What we are dealing with, in fact, is a series of variations on a common rite, a rite that has its roots behind the divisions of the Reformation and post-Reformation periods in the traditions of the undivided Western Church of the patristic and mediaeval periods.[194]

2. A common theological understanding of confirmation

The fact that the churches concerned are happy to use what is, in its fundamentals at least, the same rite indicates the existence of an underlying theological agreement about confirmation. It indicates that all these churches hold that as part of an overall process of Christian initiation it is important that there should be a rite in which those who have already received God's grace through the sacrament of baptism and are able to answer for themselves, should

- re-affirm the promises made at their baptism

- express their belief in the common faith of the Christian Church

- commit themselves to living the Christian life

- receive the laying on of hands with prayer to the end that they will be strengthened through Holy Spirit for lives of Christian discipleship within the fellowship of the Church.[195]

193 That is the significance of the sharing of the peace in the Church of England and Roman Catholic rites and is implicit in the final words of the Lutheran rite.

194 The Old Catholic Churches of the Union of Utrecht also have confirmation rites in the same tradition, but it has not proved possible to obtain details of their rites while preparing this paper. This is an area where further research is required.

195 It is interesting to note that the common use of Isaiah 11.2–3 seems to indicate a common conviction that those confirmed will share in the sevenfold messianic anointing by the Spirit of Christ himself. I have never seen this idea made explicit, but it would be an interesting topic to pursue.

It is also arguable that, like the Church of England, all the other churches involved also view confirmation as a means of grace. That is to say, if we assume that the churches concerned are serious about the prayers that are used in their rites they must believe that God will act in response to these prayers as part of his gracious activity in the lives of those who are being prayed for.

The existence of this sort of agreement about confirmation has been affirmed in a number of recent ecumenical agreements.

For example, in the Porvoo agreement of 1993 the Anglican and Lutheran churches note that both traditions practise rites of confirmation which include 'invocation of the Triune God, renewal of the baptismal profession of faith and a prayer that through the renewal of the grace of baptism the candidate may be strengthened now and forever'.[196]

An Anglican–Methodist Covenant (published 2001) likewise states that, while there are differing views about confirmation in both the Church of England and the Methodist Church, nevertheless,

> Confirmation is regarded by both churches as a means of grace within the total process of Christian initiation. For both churches, Confirmation includes the reaffirmation of the baptismal promises by the candidate, accompanied by the prayer with the laying on of hands that God will strengthen the candidate in his or her discipleship through the work of the Holy Spirit.[197]

The new agreed statement of the International Anglican–Roman Catholic Commission for Unity and Mission (IARCCUM) *Growing Together in Unity and Mission* also notes agreement about confirmation:

> In both the Anglican Communion and the Roman Catholic Church, the sacramental process of Christian initiation also includes confirmation. Common to our understanding is that confirmation is an empowerment by the Holy Spirit for unity and mission, and a public manifestation of membership in the body of Christ.[198]

It is worth noting that, although The Episcopal Church in the United States lays great stress on the idea of baptism as complete sacramental initiation, and

---

196 *Together in Mission and Unity* (London: Church House Publishing, 1993), p. 19.
197 *An Anglican–Methodist Covenant* (Peterborough/London: Methodist Publishing House/Church House Publishing, 2001), p. 41.
198 *Growing Together in Unity and Mission* (London: SPCK, 2007), p. 24.

although its confirmation rite emphasizes strongly the renewal of the covenant made at baptism,[199] nevertheless the rite still contains the traditional element of the laying on of hands by the bishop and contains the two traditional prayers:

> Strengthen, O Lord, your servant N, with your Holy Spirit; empower him for your service; and sustain him all the days of his life. Amen

or

> Defend, O Lord, your servant N, with your heavenly grace, that he may continue yours for ever, and daily increase in your Holy Spirit more and more, until he comes to your everlasting kingdom. Amen

The Episcopal Church rite does, therefore, still form part of the ecumenical convergence over confirmation.[200]

3. Confirmation and the Baptist tradition

The churches that are mentioned above as exhibiting a fundamental agreement about confirmation represent five of the major traditions of Western Christianity. One major tradition that is missing from the list, however, is the Baptist tradition. This is because for Baptists affirmation of faith, commitment to Christian discipleship, and baptism have traditionally been seen as things that properly belong together. A key reason why Baptists have had difficulty with infant baptism is because they have felt that a form of baptism that was not linked to a personal affirmation of faith and commitment to Christian discipleship was not true baptism.

In a recent contribution to informal conversations between the Church of England and the Baptist Union of Great Britain the Baptist theologian Paul Fiddes has argued that the traditional polarization between the infant and adult baptism approaches to Christian initiation can be overcome if we think in terms of the existence of two 'equivalent stories' of the journey of Christian initiation.

> If baptism is truly to be a means a means of binding Christians together

---

199 For the significance of the Baptismal Covenant in The Episcopal Church see C. Podmore, 'The Baptismal Revolution in the American Episcopal Church: Baptismal Ecclesiology and the Baptismal Covenant', *Ecclesiology* 6, 2010, pp. 8–38.

200 The TEC rite in *The Episcopal Church Book of Common Prayer* can be found at http://justus.anglican.org/resources/bcp/bcp.htm

('one baptism'), we must then compare not single moments – but journeys, and this means listening to others' stories of their journey. One journey, a Baptist experience, may be from infant blessing through Christian nurture in childhood to believers' baptism, laying on of hands for gifts of the Spirit, and then increasing use of those gifts in ministry in the world. An Anglican or Reformed journey might be from infant baptism, through Christian nurture in childhood, to public profession of faith, and laying on of hands in confirmation for gifts of the Spirit, to be used in ministry in the world.[201]

For Fiddes, recognizing these as two equivalent journeys opens up the possibility of the mutual recognition by both adult and paedo-baptists of each others' patterns of Christian initiation:

> We are in a broken situation where churches have different beliefs about baptism, owing to different interpretations of Scripture and the different paths they have taken in history. Without abandoning their convictions, Baptists might be able to value and affirm someone's whole journey of experience, and not just the moment of public profession of faith on which attention is usually fixed; they might be able gladly to recognize how God has used every stage of the journey for saving purposes. Correspondingly, those who baptize infants as well as believers (since all churches practise believers' baptism in the case of older converts) might feel more free to offer some parents the option of delaying the baptism of their child until a later age, with the alternative of a service of infant blessing.[202]

Fiddes notes, however, that in order for the idea of two equivalent journeys of Christian initiation to work, those churches that practise infant baptism need to give proper weight to confirmation, 'against the trend to downplay confirmation in favour of a single "unified rite of initiation"'.[203]

Although it can be legitimately asked how representative Paul Fiddes is of Baptists in general, his work suggests that it is possible to see confirmation as having an important part to play in the development of agreement on the subject of Christian initiation between Baptists and those churches that practise infant baptism.

---

201 P. Fiddes, 'One baptism: a Baptist contribution', in *Pushing at the Boundaries of Unity* (London: Church House Publishing, 2005), pp. 41–2.

202 *Ibid.*, p. 42.

203 *Ibid.*, pp. 55–6.

4. Confirmation and chrismation

It is important to note that confirmation can only function as the basis for wider ecumenical agreement in this way if the elements of personal affirmation of baptismal promises and personal confession of faith are seen as integral parts of confirmation. This further means that an important distinction needs to be made between confirmation and the practice of chrismation in the Orthodox churches and the Roman Catholic churches of the Eastern rite.

Confirmation and chrismation are often regarded as equivalent to each other. The *Catechism of the Catholic Church*, for example, treats them as equivalent and this has also been the position of the Church of England, reflected in the fact that those who have received Orthodox chrismation are not subsequently confirmed if they join the Church of England. It can also be argued that historically confirmation developed out of chrismation in the later Patristic period, with the laying on of hands and anointing becoming detached from the baptismal rite of which it was originally a part.

However, a case can be made out for saying that at least when the subject of chrismation is an infant it is not equivalent to confirmation. This is because when the subject of chrismation is an infant the infant receives an anointing with oil as a sign of their reception of the Holy Spirit, but no element of overt personal response is involved.

As we have seen, this element of personal response is an integral part of the rite of confirmation as it has developed in the Western Church and it is theologically very important if we take seriously what the New Testament teaches about the importance of personal faith (Mark 1.15; John 3.16; Rom. 3.25–26; 1 Pet. 3.8–9; 1 John 5.13). It is vital that, as part of the process of Christian initiation, an opportunity is provided for personal faith to be expressed by those who have reached the years of discretion. Confirmation provides that opportunity; chrismation does not and therefore the two are not exactly equivalent.

Recognition of this fact raises important questions for both the Roman Catholic Church and the Church of England which have regarded confirmation and chrismation as practically identical. A better approach to a comparison of Christian initiation in the Eastern and Western traditions might be to look at the way (or ways) in which those who are baptized as infants in the Orthodox churches receive catechesis and give expression to their commitment themselves to living out the faith into which they were baptized.

This might then provide an equivalent overall pattern of initiation, even if chrismation and confirmation are not precisely equivalent.

5. Confirmation and dialogue with Christians in the Pentecostal tradition

A key element in confirmation is that we receive the Spirit in a new way to enable us to serve God more faithfully and effectively within the fellowship of his Church. As many charismatic Anglican and Roman Catholic theologians have suggested, we can identify this fresh anointing with the Spirit with the traditional Pentecostal emphasis on the baptism of the Holy Spirit. These can be seen as two ways of describing the same reality.

In his book *Baptism* Michael Green quotes a letter from the Anglican nun Sister Margaret Magdalen that makes this point:

> For a long time I had prayed for baptism in the Spirit, and felt puzzled and grieved that God did not appear to respond to this prayer. Then, when I became an Anglican, I was confirmed. The only sense I could make of confirmation at that stage in my life, when I had been a committed Christian and indeed a missionary for many years, was to see it as part of, and all of a piece with, my baptism (which had been as a believer by immersion).

> So I prepared for confirmation as a deepening of the initial baptism, laying hold of that grace within the sacrament with firm hands. As the confirmation service proceeded, I became full of a radiant joy which simply overflowed – I couldn't contain it. I didn't sleep a wink that night because I was filled with praise and joy sometimes poured forth in tongues and sometimes took me in to a deep contemplative silence. Next day my students were awed when I began to teach them. When I asked them why they were so subdued, they told me they were afraid of the shining of my face. Like Moses I did not know I shone.

'For me,' she adds, 'that was a mighty experience (there have been others since) of the Holy Spirit, but it was part of baptism and confirmation – all one sacrament. I realized then that I had been praying with wrong expectations before. God had now answered in *his* way.' [204]

The reason why this story is worth quoting is that it shows a classic Pentecostal

---

204 M. Green, *Baptism* (London: Hodder & Stoughton, 1987), pp. 140–1.

experience taking place within the framework of the traditional practice of confirmation. Experiences like those of Sister Margaret Magdalen point us in the direction of a potentially fruitful discussion about confirmation between the Pentecostals and other churches.

In such a discussion those churches that practise confirmation might want to ask the Pentecostals what prevents them from recognizing the rite of confirmation as providing an occasion for people to receive the power and presence of the Holy Spirit into their lives in a new way. Why should they not recognize that the laying on of hands with prayer for the gift of the Spirit in confirmation is the same activity, based on the same biblical models, as the laying on of hands with prayer for the gift of the Spirit that is a key feature of Pentecostal practice?

On the other hand, the Pentecostals might want to ask those churches that practise confirmation for evidence that those who are confirmed really do receive the gift of the Spirit. Where, they might ask, are those supernatural signs of the Spirit's presence that are present in the New Testament accounts of the life of the early Church and have been a key part of Pentecostal experience? Why are experiences like those of Sister Margaret Magdalen still comparatively rare? They would challenge these churches that practise confirmation to be more open to God moving in power and to the exercise of those miraculous gifts of the Spirit referred to by St Paul in 1 Corinthians 12.4–11.

A discussion along those lines has the potential to help both sides to move beyond their traditional positions and to learn to see God working in ways that they would not normally expect.

A good example of such a dialogue is the discussion on 'Baptism in the Holy Spirit and Christian Initiation' which took place as the fifth phase of the international Pentecostal–Roman Catholic Dialogue between 1998 and 2003. The discussion, which included a sustained study of Scripture and the Fathers as well as the current positions of the two sides, did not result in an overall theological agreement about what Baptism in the Holy Spirit involves. It led instead to the recognition that there is a broad diversity of interpretation regarding baptism in the Holy Spirit within the Pentecostal and Roman Catholic traditions, as well as between them. However, both sides were able to agree that 'Baptism in the Holy Spirit is a powerful action of grace bestowed by God upon believers within the Church' and that 'during the last century the lifting up of Baptism in the Holy Spirit as part of the reality of Christ's community has been a gift to the Church'. They also agreed that the growth of the charismatic renewal movement within the Roman Catholic Church from the 1960s onwards had allowed Pentecostals and Roman Catholics to see each other in a more positive light.

An interesting part of the report is the section that deals with the interpretation of Baptism in the Holy Spirit within the Roman Catholic Church. One school of interpretation, represented by *The Malines Document* of 1974, holds that Baptism in the Holy Spirit should be seen as part of the fullness of Christian sacramental initiation through baptism, confirmation and the Eucharist. The other approach, represented by the paper *The Spirit Gives Life*, approved by the German Bishops Conference in 1987, holds that a Christian does not possess the Spirit in a static manner, but should be open to 'occasional renewals' or 'new sendings forth of the Spirit' alongside the continuous indwelling of the Spirit resulting from baptism and confirmation. This internal Roman Catholic discussion might prove a useful resource for other churches with a strong emphasis on the impartation of the Spirit at baptism and confirmation, as they seek to make sense theologically of the experience of charismatic renewal.[205]

6. Areas of continuing ecumenical disagreement about confirmation

So far in this chapter we have demonstrated that there is substantial agreement about confirmation among those churches that practise the rite and we have suggested that confirmation provides a potentially fruitful basis for dialogue with Baptists and Pentecostals. In the final part of this chapter we shall go on look at areas of continuing ecumenical disagreement about confirmation. Before we do that, however, we need to deal with a red herring.

The red herring in question is the view that one still encounters in some Anglican circles that the Methodist and United Reformed churches see confirmation simply as a means of entry into Church membership. This is not so.

As we have already seen, it is true that that the Methodist and United Reformed churches have rites that bring together confirmation and reception into membership in a single service. However, a closer examination of their respective rites shows that reception into membership is only one element of the service and the overall understanding of confirmation reflected in their rites is the same as that of the Church of England.

205 The report of the discussion can be found on the Pro Unione website at http://www.prounione.urbe.it/dia-int/pe-rc/doc/e_pe-rc_5–6.html

Furthermore, if we ask what 'membership' actually means in the Methodist Church and the United Reformed Church we find that it means responsible mature participation in the life of the local Christian community, and this is precisely what confirmation has been traditionally seen to lead to in the Church of England and in the Roman Catholic Church.[206] Thus, by linking confirmation to reception into membership, the Methodist and United Reformed churches are actually taking the same approach to confirmation as the Church of England.

If we dispense with this red herring we find that there are three points of continuing disagreement between the churches over confirmation.

1. Is it right to describe confirmation as a sacrament?

The Roman Catholic Church is clear that confirmation is a sacrament. The *Catechism of the Catholic Church* declares explicitly: 'Christ instituted the sacraments of the new law. There are seven: Baptism, Confirmation (or Chrismation), the Eucharist, Penance, the Anointing of the Sick, Holy Orders and Matrimony.'[207]

In their official teaching, the Church of England, the Churches of the Lutheran tradition, the Methodist Church, the United Reformed Church and the Moravian Church do not recognize confirmation as a sacrament. This is because they follow the consensus that emerged on the Protestant side at the Reformation that there are only two sacraments properly so called, baptism and the Eucharist. This position is clearly set out, for example, in Article XXV of the Thirty-nine Articles of Religion of the Church of England: 'There are two Sacraments ordained of Christ our Lord in the Gospel, that is to say, Baptism and the Supper of the Lord.'

> Those five commonly called Sacraments, that is to say, Confirmation, Penance, Orders, Matrimony, and Extreme Unction, are not to be counted for Sacraments of the Gospel, being such as have grown partly of the corrupt following of the Apostles, partly are states of life allowed in the Scriptures; but yet have not the like nature of Sacraments with

---

206 It is interesting to note, for example, that the disciplines to which members of the Methodist Church commit themselves are essentially those that would be expected of those confirmed in the Church of England (with the addition of an explicit commitment to giving financially to the church).

207 *Catechism of the Catholic Church*, 1210, p. 276.

Baptism and the Lord's Supper, for that they have not any visible sign or ceremony ordained of God.

There is a genuine disagreement here that shows no sign of being resolved, but it is important not to overestimate its importance. As we have seen, there is a consensus among the churches that practise confirmation that it is a genuine means of grace. One might even be able to push the consensus further and say that they might be able to agree that confirmation has a 'sacramental' character in the sense that the prayer and the laying on of hands in confirmation conform to Peter Lombard's definition of a sacrament as an 'outward and visible sign of an inward and invisible grace'.

Where the churches differ is over the question of whether Christ himself instituted confirmation in the same way that he instituted baptism and the Eucharist, or whether confirmation was a rite that developed later in the history of the Church without explicit dominical authority. Both sides in this debate are agreed that a key part of the definition of a sacrament is that Christ instituted it, where they differ is over the question of which rites fit this requirement.

The *Catechism of the Catholic Church*, for instance, declares that, following on from Christ's impartation of the Spirit on Easter Sunday and on the Day of Pentecost:

> the apostles, in fulfilment of Christ's will, imparted to the newly baptized by the laying on of hands the gift of the Spirit that completes the grace of Baptism. For this reason in the *Letter to the Hebrews* the doctrine concerning Baptism and the laying on of hands is listed among the first elements of Christian instruction. The imposition of hands is rightly recognized by the Catholic tradition as the origin of the sacrament of Confirmation, which in a certain way perpetuates the grace of Pentecost in the Church.[208]

Christians from other traditions, however, would want to raise questions about the hermeneutical move made in this quotation. They would acknowledge that the verses referred to in this quotation (Acts 8.15–17, 19.5–6; Heb. 6.2) do point to the practice of the laying on of hands existing in New Testament times. They might also be willing to say that this happened in accordance with Christ's will. Nevertheless, they would want to ask in what sense the laying on of hands mentioned in New Testament times can be seen as the 'origin' of the

---

208 *Ibid.*, 1288, p. 290.

sacrament of confirmation, given that historically a rite of confirmation separate from baptism only began to emerge in the Western Church at the end of the Patristic period as a result of a long process of historical development. Given the late development of confirmation, they would say, it is difficult to see how it can claim the same sort of direct dominical authorization as baptism and the Eucharist.

Where ecumenical progress might be possible, however, is in a mutual recognition that even if confirmation was not directly instituted by Christ himself in the same way that baptism and the Eucharist were, nevertheless the existence of confirmation should not be regarded as an accident, but should be seen as a gift of God that came into existence as part of God's providential ordering of the history of his people. In this way its God-given character could be recognized without having to make difficult claims about the meaning of the laying on of hands in the New Testament texts.

2. Who is the proper minister of the rite?

In the Church of England the confirming minister has to be a bishop. The Roman Catholic Church holds that a bishop is the normal minister of confirmation in the Western rite, but that he may delegate the administration of confirmation to a priest for 'grave reasons'. The Lutheran, EKD, Methodist, United Reformed, Church of Scotland and Moravian churches, on the other hand, practise purely presbyteral confirmation.

The *Catechism of the Catholic Church* explains why the bishop is the normal minister of confirmation: 'Bishops are the successors of the apostles. They have received the fullness of the sacrament of Holy Orders. The administration of this sacrament by them demonstrates clearly that its effect is to unite those who receive it more closely to the Church, to her apostolic origins and to her mission of bearing witness to Christ.'[209]

For the Church of England, the reason why it is appropriate that a bishop should confirm is because this expresses the role of the bishop as the principal minister of Christian initiation in an episcopally ordered church. As the Church of England report on Christian initiation *On the Way* puts it:

> In an episcopally ordered Church the bishop is the chief minister of the whole process of Christian initiation and is integral to its practice. This

---

209 *Ibid.*, 1313, p. 296.

finds expression in a number of features of current practice: the requirement of episcopal confirmation (Canon B27; B15A); the canonical requirement that the bishop be given notice of an adult baptism (Canon B24.2); the final say resting with the bishop over a refusal to baptize an infant (Canon B22.2), and over any attempt to bar a baptized person from receiving Communion (Canon B16).[210]

To put it simply, the bishop is responsible for overseeing the whole process of Christian initiation, although he may delegate parts of the initiation process to his presbyters and deacons, and the point at which this overall responsibility is symbolized is in his role as the minister of confirmation.

Those churches that practise presbyteral confirmation, on the other hand, would see confirming people as part of the normal work of the local minister, just like presiding at the Eucharist or baptizing. In addition, in the churches of the Lutheran tradition, and in the EKD in general, preparing people for confirmation is viewed as a central part of the catechetical responsibility of the local minister and it is therefore seen as proper that the same minister should confirm those that he or she has prepared.

3. Can the Church of England recognize presbyteral confirmation in other churches?

The Lutheran, Methodist, United Reformed and Moravian churches recognize one another's confirmations and confirmations performed in the Church of England and in the Roman Catholic Church. A confirmation rite is a confirmation rite whether performed by a bishop or a presbyter. What matters, as far they are concerned, is that the proper elements for a confirmation rite should be in place.

The Roman Catholic Church does not recognize the confirmations of any of the other churches just mentioned or of the Church of England. This because it believes that confirmation is a sacramental act that can only be performed by validly ordained ministers acting on behalf of bishops in apostolic succession, a condition that none of the confirmations performed in these other churches meets in the Roman Catholic view. Consequently the Roman Catholic Church practices the presbyteral (re-)confirmation of adults confirmed in another church who are received into communion.[211] The reason, incidentally, why it

---

210 *On the Way* (London: Church House Publishing, 1995), p. 107.
211 *Catechism of the Catholic Church*, 1289, p. 296.

can recognize the baptisms of other churches even though it does not recognize their confirmations is because it holds that baptism can be performed by a lay person,[212] and so the issue of a valid ministry does not arise.

The Church of England recognizes for its own purposes confirmations performed by bishops whose orders it recognizes (this includes the bishops of the Roman Catholic Church). It also generally recognizes presbyteral confirmations performed in the Roman Catholic Church on behalf of a bishop, using oil consecrated by the bishop, and presbyteral chrismation performed in the churches of the Orthodox tradition, again using chrism consecrated by the bishop.[213] However, the Church of England does not recognize any other presbyteral confirmation, such as those performed in churches of the Lutheran, Methodist, United Reformed or Moravian traditions, and it practises episcopal (re-)confirmation of those who have been thus confirmed in cases where individuals coming from any of those churches wish to become Readers or to be ordained.

But what happens to the logic of this position when joint confirmation is brought into the picture? Joint services of confirmation may be held in Local Ecumenical Partnerships: the candidates are confirmed by the ministers of two or more of the churches involved in the particular LEP (which may not necessarily be a single-congregation type of LEP, but may, for example, be a local covenant partnership). As far as the Church of England is concerned, joint confirmation means the holding of joint Anglican–Methodist, Anglican–United Reformed Church or Anglican–Moravian confirmation services.

In a joint confirmation the confirming minister from the Church of England is always a bishop in line with standard Anglican ecclesiology. In the case of the other churches it is the appropriate minister in terms of their normal practice. This usually means the local Methodist, United Reformed Church, or Moravian minister who has responsibility for the LEP. However, the Circuit Superintendent or District Chairman may sometimes act for the Methodist Church, or the Synod Moderator for the United Reformed Church.

Canonical provision for the holding of such services is given in Canon B 44.4 (1) (e) and 44.2 which state that a bishop who has agreed to Church of England participation in an LEP may '. . . make provision for the holding in that area of joint services with any other participating Church, including services of

---

212 *Ibid.*, 1256, p. 285.

213 This has been the generally accepted interpretation of Canon B15a although the validity of this interpretation has recently been questioned.

baptism and confirmation', provided that 'he is satisfied that the rite and the elements to be used are not contrary to, nor indicative of any departure from, the doctrine of the Church of England in any essential matter'.

In summary, from a Church of England point of view, joint confirmation means a service of confirmation taking place under the provisions of Canon B 44 in which a bishop of the Church of England confirms candidates from an LEP together with a Methodist, URC, or Moravian minister using a rite which he believes to be agreeable to the doctrine of the Church of England.

The canonical provision for joint confirmation calls into question any suggestion that the Church of England holds that only bishops or presbyters acting on behalf of bishops can confirm. The fact that the Church of England takes part in joint confirmations in which presbyters not acting on behalf of a bishop confirm seems to indicate that this cannot be a cast-iron rule. Joint confirmation would make no sense as *joint* confirmation if the Church of England believed that in these circumstances only the bishop was truly confirming.

The Church of England has been challenged about its practice of (re-) confirmation by the EKD via the Commission overseeing the implementation of the Meissen Agreement of 1991 between the EKD and the Church of England and by the Methodist Church via the Joint Implementation Commission. The Church of England will therefore need to give some serious attention to this issue in the not-too-distant future. It is on this issue that the question of the ecumenical significance of confirmation, explored in this chapter, really begins to bite.

6

The minister of confirmation

Christopher Hill

The English Reformation and the seventeenth century

By the time of the sixteenth-century Reformation in Western Europe the Church – conservative and radical – had inherited a rite of 'confirmation' essentially separated from the sacrament of baptism, given and to be given a variety of meanings.[214] Its normal minister was the bishop, the minister of baptism having become normally the parish priest. There had, however, been some known exceptions to the episcopal norm illustrated, for example, in the Decree of Clement IV in 1351 which recognized the Armenian (and Eastern) tradition of chrismation by the priest as the equivalent of Western confirmation (a debatable point, but it is not my point here). The decree (to be repeated by the Council of Florence eighty years later) begins by reiterating that the normal minister is the bishop, justifying this with reference to Acts 8.14–17. But, after stating that anointing was the equivalent to the laying on of hands, there is an interesting caveat: 'Nevertheless, we read that sometimes through a dispensation of the apostolic See for a reasonable and very urgent cause a simple priest has administered the sacrament of confirmation with chrism prepared by the bishop.' Equally, St Thomas Aquinas taught that the Pope can grant priests the privilege of administering confirmation. Thus when the Council of Trent anathematized those who denied that the bishop was the 'ordinary' minister of confirmation, its language explicitly *did not condemn* the view that priests could be extraordinary ministers of confirmation.[215]

214 For example, the modern Roman Catholic understanding of confirmation as the 'ordination' of the laity, as if the baptismal and corporate priesthood did not achieve this.

215 This is the current position in the practice and law of the Roman Catholic Church. In 1946 Pius XII granted indults for priestly confirmations followed in 1971 by Paul VI. While the bishop remains the 'ordinary' (*originarius*) minister of confirmation, all parish priests may confirm and all priests in a situation where there is danger of death.

To this tradition Archbishop Cranmer made no significant change with the advent of the First Prayer Book of 1549, *other* than an emphasis in the opening rubric of the Catechism (which precedes the Confirmation Service) on knowing the Lord's Prayer, the Ten Commandments and the Catechism itself. This was not, however, wholly new and followed mediaeval precedent. The third rubric of the Catechism is equally mediaeval in explaining the meaning of the rite: 'that they may receive strength and defence against all temptations to sin and the assaults of the world and the devil' at just the age when 'by the frailty of their own flesh, partly by the assaults of the world and the devil, they begin to be in danger to fall into sin'. It also noted that confirmation was not essential to salvation – Trent had said the opposite in 1547 but that decree had not been published. The rite of confirmation itself is brief. There is a prayer for the Spirit and the sevenfold gifts which closely followed the Latin Sarum Rite (the predominant but not the sole rite in use in England prior to the Reformation). The candidates were signed with the sign of the cross and the bishop laid his hands upon the heads of the candidates. The use of oil of chrism, however, was discontinued in 1552, the signing was omitted and the prayer for the sevenfold gifts of the Spirit changed from 'send down . . . thy Holy Ghost . . .' to 'strengthen them . . . with the Holy Ghost . . . ', paradoxically making the rite more mediaeval rather than less. This remained the text in 1662, the earlier pre-catechismal rubrics now standing as a Preface to the confirmation service to be read by the bishop or another minister. The references to pubescent sin were, however, decently removed. Importantly, 1662 introduced a brief renewal of baptismal promises, to which the candidates had to assent audibly. The 1928 revision[216] of the Prayer Book (which never received the necessary Parliamentary approval for it to have formal authority) introduced a new preface referring to Acts 8 and speaking of a special gift of the Spirit. It also (optionally) expanded the renewal of baptismal vows. *All* the Prayer Books concluded the rite with a prayer said by the bishop which stated: following 'the example of thy holy apostles, we have now laid our hands . . . '.[217] The minister of confirmation in all the English Prayer Book rites remained exclusively the bishop.

Though the ritual changes to confirmation were relatively conservative during the sixteenth and seventeenth centuries in England, the cataclysmic religious

216 The 1928 Prayer Book obviously does not belong to the seventeenth century. But I include it here for completeness as it was essentially a conservative revision of a seventeenth-century rite. Contemporary English Anglican liturgy is dealt with below.

217 For a survey of Anglican Communion developments see J. D. C. Fisher, *Confirmation: Then and Now*, Alcuin Club Collections No. 60 (London: SPCK, 1978).

clash of the English Civil War and the Commonwealth period meant that in religious *practice* confirmation was very rarely administered (and only illegally) from 1645 to the Restoration in 1661. The debates with the Puritans (whether inside or outside the established Church) included whether or not 'confirmation' was scripturally apostolic. There was a considerable controversial literature. Richard Hooker, as always judicious, is careful to not make 'confirmation any part of that power which has always belonged only unto bishops because in some places the custom was that presbyters might also confirm *in the absence of a bishop* [my emphasis]; albeit for the most part none but only bishops were therefore the allowed ministers'.[218]

Hooker had earlier defended episcopal confirmation as both scriptural and patristic and also discussed the severance of confirmation from baptism, the readmission of baptized heretics by 'confirmation', the accusation that 'confirmation' only came by way of the False Decretals, and the danger of episcopal confirmation denigrating baptism. The Puritans continued to be suspicious of episcopal confirmation as both 'popish and peevish'. It is also a fact that not every bishop in the sixteenth and seventeenth centuries was zealous to administer confirmation. Archbishop Whitgift of Canterbury wrote to his fellow bishops in the Canterbury Province in 1591: 'I am very sorry to hear that my brethren the bishops . . . do so generally begin to neglect to confirm children.'

Most of the seventeenth-century Caroline Divines wrote in defence of episcopal confirmation and its ancient usage (oil and the sign of the cross): for example John Cosin, Joseph Hall, Hammond, L'Estrange, Jeremy Taylor and Edward Bougham. But there is also the fine Puritan testimony of Richard Baxter. Baxter was confirmed in a churchyard as a boy, the whole countryside running to be 'bishopped'. Baxter lamented its casualness and lack of devotion or interrogation in the faith. His criticism of what was a continued (bad) mediaeval practice of hearing that a bishop was in the district and seeking 'confirmation' is sharp. Yet he ends by saying: 'this was the old, careless practice of this *excellent* (my emphasis) duty of confirmation'.

The immediate concern of the restored Anglican bishops in 1661 was with baptism itself. This is reflected in a new rite for the Public Baptism of adults found in the 1662 Prayer Book. Many people had not been baptized at all during the Commonwealth period and the bishops attempted to remedy this with the new rite. Importantly for our subject, the minister was required to give

218 *Laws of Ecclesiastical Polity*, Book VII, Ch. iv.4.

notice to the bishop of such adult baptismal candidates; this remains in the Prayer Book and is also enjoined by Canon B 24, echoing (faintly) the patristic norm that the bishop was the proper minister of baptism (and so also of what later became 'confirmation').

The English Anglican tradition up to the Restoration and since has therefore understood the bishop to be the normal minister of confirmation rather than the presbyter. Theologians such as Hooker, however, recognized proper exceptions to the norm.

The eighteenth and nineteenth centuries: decline and renewal

In this short summary only a few indications can be offered of a long and complicated pastoral, evangelistic and theological development. There is evidence in the eighteenth century of both heroic practice and serious neglect. In *Confirmation in the Anglican Communion*, S. L. Ollard produced a serious study of diocesan visitation articles and other records from the year 1500 to 1850. His extended essay was part of the semi-official two-volume study *Confirmation: Historical and Doctrinal* published over 80 years ago.[219] Ollard was able to show from research in a number of dioceses that, in the first quarter of the eighteenth century, in some dioceses the episcopal articles of Visitation contain no reference to confirmation. In others, however, questions are asked and people are to be prepared for confirmation and communion.

In the 1662 Prayer Book the final rubric of the confirmation service, which governs admission to Holy Communion, had had to be altered. Prior to 1662 confirmation was necessary for admission to communion. During the Commonwealth, where confirmation had been abolished by the Parliamentarians, the vast majority of the population were unconfirmed; so the rule was altered. Confirmation was still required, but those 'ready and desirous to be confirmed' could also be admitted to communion. Sometimes episcopal visitation articles show that clergy thought admission to communion was the *equivalent* of confirmation; for example, of 423 returns to Archbishop Herring of York in 1743 only 15 report unconfirmed communicants (the question being asked) but the general answers indicate that many priests thought confirmation unnecessary once people had been admitted to communion. However before we are too pessimistic about pastoralia in the eighteenth-century Church of England, we should note that Archbishop Herring believed

219 S. L. Ollard, *Confirmation in the Anglican Communion* (London: SPCK, 1926).

he had in fact confirmed 'about twenty thousand people' in that year. These large numbers *might* reflect episcopal neglect under his predecessor Archbishop Blackburne. Yet even under the neglectful regime of the scandalous Archbishop Blackburne, Bishop Benson of *Gloucester* had confirmed over three days no less than 8,922 persons in Halifax and Ripponden in the West Riding of Yorkshire in 1737.[220] It was noted that he confirmed the candidates 'by only two at a time, with great devotion and solemnity'. The point being made by this surprising comment was that Bishop Benson confirmed candidates individually, by laying on a hand on each candidate's head, rather than what may have been the negligent practice of simply spreading out episcopal hands *towards* a group of candidates.

As the century wore on, however, the new industrial towns outstripped the pastoral and legal capacity of the Church of England to minister to them. Confirmation (and any regular Anglican worship) became rarer proportionally to the new urban populations. Nevertheless the situation varied considerably. Where Methodism flourished Anglicanism became proportionally less strong, at least until the Evangelical and Anglo-Catholic revivals. It was the 'ritualistic' parishes of the second phase of the Oxford Movement that made most gains in the poverty-stricken urban slums. And with the ritualists came a high doctrine (and practice) of confirmation. Yet it was not only the Anglo-Catholics who sought a reform in the practice of confirmation. A privately published account by an Evangelical clergyman (William Cecil) in 1833 describes two highly disorderly confirmations, one of five and a half hours of irreverence in Ely diocese.[221] Evangelical reforms followed in the 1820s in Gloucester and Lichfield dioceses and then with Charles Sumner at Winchester, followed by Samuel Wilberforce at Oxford.

Once the large, chaotic and irreverent confirmation services became a thing of the past and the revival of pastoral visitations of parishes got underway in the second half of the nineteenth century, the necessity of *parish* confirmations became apparent and normal. Though this required much more episcopal time, it was now more possible because of the railway services throughout the country. As a consequence, *more* bishops were required to administer confirmation pastorally and decently. One very important but neglected reason for the growth in the number of suffragan sees in the Church of England from the second half of the nineteenth century onwards has been the revival of pastoral and parochial confirmations. Yet at no point has there been a

220 *Ibid.*, p. 198 and pp. 224–31 for the visitational evidence.
221 *Ibid.*, pp. 213–14.

serious proposal that the minister of confirmation should be other than the bishop.

Contemporary Church of England services

To complete the summary of liturgical history, I need to briefly mention the *Alternative Service Book* of 1980, now superseded by *Common Worship: Initiation Services*. In the *Alternative Service Book*, and even more strikingly in *Common Worship*, there is a return to a patristic pattern of a holistic rite of Christian Initiation. Confirmation is increasingly administered within a pattern of Baptism, Confirmation and Holy Communion, and there are usually some baptisms at most confirmations – this at least has been my experience in the two rather different dioceses of Lichfield and Guildford.

It is not surprising that with this strongly 'patristic' Liturgy of Initiation the bishop remains the 'President' of the rite. Though this does not inhibit *some* delegation, for example the signing with the cross and baptism, 'confirmation' remains exclusively episcopal. For Anglicans, the bishop has historically always been the minister of confirmation; the bishop is now becoming once again a regular minister of especially adult baptism – my starting point.

Anglican practice: episcopal confirmations, their ecumenical status; canon law

The consistent and unbroken Anglican practice (in the Church of England) has maintained exclusively episcopal confirmation. Yet this has never been raised to the status of an essential belief. As we have seen, Hooker strongly defended episcopal confirmations while admitting there had been exceptions in history. The danger of elaborating a theology about confirmation, as separate from baptism, has been seen. St Jerome would have disliked the Anglo-Catholic argument just as strongly as its more modern opponents.[222] Moreover, there

222 Jerome, *Dial.adv. Lucif. Vii*, 'I do not deny that this is the custom of the church that the Bishop should rush about (*excurrat*) to those who have been baptized by Presbyters or Deacons far from larger cities, to call down the Holy Spirit by the laying on of hands. This is done in many places, yet is done rather for the glory of the Bishop, than from any pressure of necessity. If the Holy Ghost only descends at the mighty imprecation of a Bishop, they are most unfortunate who live in farms or villages, or who happen to die in remote spots after being baptized by Presbyters or Deacons before the Bishop can discover them. The whole salvation of the Church depends upon the Bishop's self-importance. Unless he is given some exceptional power which outshines everyone else, there will be as many schisms as there are Bishops.'

are ecumenical reasons of *praxis* that underscore that the issue of presbyteral confirmation is not a church-dividing matter. It was agreed in the *Porvoo* discussions that presbyteral confirmation was not a matter that would be an obstacle to closer communion. In *Together in Mission and Ministry*, the Porvoo Churches have agreed:

> In all our traditions *baptism* is followed by a rite of *confirmation*. We recognize two practices in our churches, both of which have precedents in earlier centuries: in Anglican churches, confirmation administered by the bishop; in the Nordic and Baltic churches, confirmation usually administered by a local priest. In all our churches this includes invocation of the Triune God, renewal of the baptismal profession of faith and a prayer that through the renewal of the grace of baptism the candidate may be strengthened now and for ever.

The Reuilly Statement *Called to Witness and Service* is not explicit at this point, but speaks about the baptized being called 'to a new life of faith, to daily repentance and discipleship', echoing the *Leuenberg Agreement*. This reflects the less homogenous traditions of confirmation in the French Protestant churches. The *Meissen Agreement* between the Church of England and the Evangelische Kirche in Deutschland speaks of baptism and the Holy Spirit without reference to confirmation.

Anglican practice has consistently been to recognize and not repeat Roman Catholic confirmations when a Roman Catholic person becomes an Anglican. Similarly, Orthodox chrismation has been accepted, though such chrismation was never in reality the equivalent of the (separated) Western rite of confirmation. Confirmation by unction is referred to specifically in Canon B 15 in this context. In the case of Roman Catholics, this provision will include those confirmed by priests under delegated episcopal authority and, in the case of Orthodox, presbyteral chrismation with oil consecrated by the bishop.

A very recent Opinion of the Legal Advisory Commission (2009) has confirmed this interpretation of the Canons in relation to Canon C 4 which requires ordinands 'to have been baptized and confirmed'. The Commission also considered Canon B 27 (Of Confirmation) which requires the bishop (or a bishop lawfully deputed) to minister confirmation. The Legal Advisory Commission considered the implications of Canons B 43 and B 44 and their Code of Practice in relation to the above and were clear that the legal provision for joint confirmations (whatever hesitations some may have about their theological meaning) implied that non-episcopally administered confirmations should be regarded as confirmations. The Commission also considered Canon B 28 which refers to the reception of persons from other churches and is the only canon *specifically* to speak of 'episcopal confirmation'. The Canon however deals with candidates from the Orthodox and Roman Catholic churches – unction is referred to as an alternative to the laying on of hands and was introduced into the *draft* Canon specifically with the Orthodox and Roman Catholic churches in mind. Confirmation in this Canon refers to confirmation as practised where the bishop remains the originating, ordinary, minister of the sacraments of initiation, but in which there can be delegation to a presbyter. The Commission's formal opinion is therefore that 'episcopal confirmation' in Canon B 28 and confirmation in Canon C 4 should be interpreted as including confirmation under the authority of a bishop, and that such an interpretation accords with the original drafting of the Canons as explained by the then Canon E. W. Kemp (later Bishop of Chichester) and with the understanding of Canon B 28 as interpreted by the Council for Christian Unity which has been followed in many dioceses for a number of years.

The ecumenical question about baptism and confirmation

On the basis of the holistic understanding of Christian initiation that I have argued for in this chapter, it is not good sacramental theology to think of confirmation as conveying a *separate* gift of the Holy Spirit. Biblically and patristically the Holy Spirit belongs with baptism, but baptism understood precisely in the holistic biblical and patristic way that I have outlined – that is, including catechesis, but also renunciation of evil, profession of faith, washing with water, laying on of hands signifying the strength of the Spirit (with or without an anointing) and the completion of initiation in the Eucharist with its missional dimension of being sent out.

The ecumenical question for the future is whether *any* Christian tradition has a genuinely holistic understanding of Christian initiation and whether the 'narrowing' of the meaning of baptism to the water bath and accompanying sacramental formula is not seriously constricting of the biblical and patristic meaning of baptism which includes more than one element. I can express this interesting ecumenical question in a rather neutral way by arguing from a major contribution to the Church of England/Baptist Conversations: 'One Baptism. Towards Mutual Recognition by Anglicans and Baptists. A Baptist Contribution.'[223]

223 See *Pushing at the Boundaries of Unity: Anglicans and Baptists in Conversation* (London: Church House Publishing, 2005).

This paper argues – as I read it – for an understanding of the complete process of Christian initiation as a journey, a *process* in which the water-bath by the Church in the Triune Name is an essential but not isolated part. Essential too is a *personal* profession of living faith and repentance, but in the face of the *universal* Church. Essential too is the recognition of God's prevenient grace; essential also is the invocation and celebration of the renewing power of the Holy Spirit. The order and manner of expression of these elements has varied in the Christian history, not least between anabaptists and infant-baptists. But the recognition of process and varied ways within an integrated whole, the *one* Baptism of faith, seems the most enlightening place to start our dialogue. The question of which minister – bishop or presbyter? – is important but is secondary to this. Nevertheless, as our dialogue about episcopacy continues, the more the bishop is seen as evangelist, missionary and pastor, the more his or her relation to an integrated process of Christian initiation, that is to say the wholeness of baptism as a process, becomes important. Nevertheless, just as baptism has been delegated to the presbyterate for centuries, it is not unreasonable to respect traditions in which the separated rite of confirmation is usually delegated to parish pastors.

The minister of confirmation – a question

The question which arises for the Church of England in considering the status of the confirmations of the Methodist Church, the Evangelische Kirche in Deutschland (EKD) (and also the Nordic and Baltic Churches which, though episcopal, practise confirmations by pastors as the norm) is how the Anglican (and Roman Catholic and Orthodox) emphasis on the bishop as the proper/originating minister of Christian initiation – very obvious in the *Common Worship Initiation Services*, where the rites presided over by the bishop are the 'norm' – could continue to be affirmed and recognized without making the issue church dividing. The fragmentation of the single rite of Christian initiation in the West, which Anglicans, Baptists, Lutherans, Methodists, Reformed, Roman Catholics all inherit may, I suggest, mean an acknowledgement that none of these traditions has a 'perfect' practice or theology of initiation. In which case, the Church of England might wish to recommend to the Meissen Churches and to the Methodist Church that some reference to those exercising an *episkope* wider than the congregation would be highly desirable – initiation is into the membership of the whole Church not to a single congregation. At the same time there would need to be some recognition that their present practice is historically understandable and acceptable in the sense of not having to be 'repeated'. With Richard Hooker, we would be recognizing exceptions to episcopal confirmation in the absence of a bishop. Such an acceptance of the non-church-dividing character of our different practices in terms of the minister of confirmation can be argued more persuasively from the liturgical fact that the actual rites of confirmation in the Meissen, Porvoo and Methodist Churches are very close indeed to our own (at least today) and that all of us, in liturgical revision, are very much closer to a holistic, patristic pattern of stages of Christian discipleship, celebrated in a single culminating Rite of Initiation. The Methodist rite of confirmation is almost identical to our own. The last but two Meissen Theological Conferences demonstrated the convergence and similarities between the EKD's liturgical practice in confirmation and our own, particularly the use of the prayer for the sevenfold gifts of the Holy Spirit, one of the most ancient liturgical prayers known to the Church. A church's intention is discerned in its formal liturgical rites. To argue that the rite of confirmation can be validly administered only by a bishop would also be to fly in the face of known liturgical history from the patristic period onwards. Nevertheless, the link with the wider Church through a minister of wider *episkope* remains something we should press upon our ecumenical partners as part of the true meaning of Christian initiation into the whole Church of God.

7

The rites of Christian initiation – a bishop's theological reflections on liturgical practice

Stephen Platten

Introduction

The publication of the *Common Worship* volume *Festivals* marked the completion of the *Common Worship* project and the provision of authorized liturgical texts for this present generation in the Church of England. There is an understandable resistance within both the Liturgical Commission and the House of Bishops to any revisiting of the liturgy in the near future. Nevertheless, there are still calls to revise further. Nowhere are those calls more frequent than with the rites of Christian initiation. There are perhaps three main causes of tension. First, some believe the present rites to be too unwieldy; there are simply too many words both for regular churchgoers and for the unchurched. Secondly, there is an increasing feeling that the material can often appear to be marginal to the unchurched culture in which we live. Thirdly, many believe that the relationship of baptism to confirmation has still not been squarely faced and that there are theological and pastoral anomalies because of this. The following reflections focus on these issues and attempt to identify more sharply precisely where these tensions surface.

1. The social context

Let us begin with two different experiences. Both are actual cases in point and the contrast is between the content and pattern of the rite in each case. The first case suggests quite sharply a 'lack of fit' between pastoral response and theological/ecclesiological intentions.[224] This first example is set in an aspiring residential suburb on the north-west edge of a Northern town. The church door and main pathway face directly (and tellingly) towards the local hospice which cares for the terminally ill. The task of the Church of God in preparing us all for our mortality could not be more clearly focused. In the season of the resurrection, there is a parish Eucharist. Half an hour after the conclusion of the Eucharist there is then a service of holy baptism. There are three candidates – all infants. The total congregation numbers about fifty, only two of whom are part of the regular worshipping congregation. The rite begins with the introductory words which conclude:

> People of God, will you welcome these children and uphold them in their new life in Christ?

This is followed immediately by the questions to the godparents:

> Will you pray for them [the children], draw them by your example into the community of faith and walk with them in the way of Christ?

> In baptism these children begin their journey in faith,
> You speak for them today,
> Will you care for them,
> And help them to take their place
> Within the life and witness of Christ's Church?

Then follows the questions and answers of 'The Decision', reaching their sharpest point with the exchange:

> Do you submit to Christ as Lord?
> *I submit to Christ.*[225]

In the context of a church one-third full – much emptier than at the immediately preceding Eucharist – the full irony of these questions may reveal themselves to us. How can we frame them within this rite to make sense of what we were doing and to avoid arrant hypocrisy? After all there are virtually none of the regular worshippers present. It gets no easier as the rite proceeds. Towards the end of the service we reflect:

---

224 Cf. W. Carr, *Brief Encounters* (London: SPCK, 1985), especially Ch. 5. Carr makes some important points about the relationship of pastoral practice to a theoretical ecclesiology.

225 The House of Bishops has authorized less direct questions to be used, as in the Alternative Service Book. See *Common Worship: Christian Initiation* (London: Church House Publishing, 2006), pp. 112, 168.

> As they grow up, they will need the help and encouragement of the Christian community . . . As part of the Church of Christ, we all have a duty to support them by prayer, example and teaching.

Where is this Christian 'community', and how does this rite [of specifically *Christian* initiation] make sense in this context? Perhaps we might even ask if the rite is too *ambitious* in what it aims to encompass.

In his helpful review of David Thompson's *Baptism, Church and Society in Modern Britain*, Jeremy Morris quotes Thompson on just this dilemma:

> How far has the wish to recover some of the significance attached to baptism in the patristic period, with its greater sense of the Church as a separated society, necessarily made it more difficult for the Church to seem to welcome everyone who comes?[226]

Morris points out that Thompson's argument shows how a 'two-pronged movement both affirming sacramentalism and the significance of personal faith (briefly, a movement in part facilitated but not ultimately effected by declaratory views of baptism) if anything reinforced, rather than undercut, this growing gap between Church and society'.[227]

This very point is, perhaps, emphasized by the Liturgical Commission's own commentary on the *Common Worship* baptism rite. Within the section headed 'A theological framework', the commentary notes as its first point that baptism involves '*separation* from this world – that is, the world alienated from God, and [secondly] *reception* into a universal community centred on God'.[228]

One can hardly fault the theological argument which continues by stressing how children can grow into the fullness of the pattern of Christ's life within a community whose mission it is to serve in the power of God's Spirit in Christ's action of redeeming the world. Undoubtedly this was the vision (if not explicitly stated) of that suburban parish. An 'open' baptism policy is intended, but the impact of the words of the liturgy is to emphasize the gulf between

---

226 D. Thompson, *Baptism, Church and Society in Modern Britain: From the Evangelical Revival to 'Baptism, Eucharist and Ministry'* (Milton Keynes: Paternoster, 2005), p. xvi.

227 J. Morris, FOAG Paper, CCU/FO/07/20, p. 4.

228 *Common Worship: Christian Initiation* (London: Church House Publishing, 2006), p. 319.

communities instead of offering a model where there is a clear and safe bridge across that gulf.[229]

The gulf will not always seem quite as stark. The second case is a baptism and confirmation at a college chapel in one of the ancient universities. In the context of Haydn's *Missa Brevis* with anthems by Jonathan Dove and Morten Lauridzen, along with a substantial choir and congregation, it all feels very different, as indeed it may in a cathedral baptism and confirmation service set up as a *staged rite*. Here the two communities coalesce to a degree. Here too the sense of the Christian life as a journey is much clearer. Initiation is no longer an abrupt confrontation between two apparently segregated communities.

2. Is baptism the beginning and end of Christian initiation?

In the volumes that make up *A Companion to Common Worship*, edited by the liturgist Paul Bradshaw, a brief history of the development of the rites of Christian initiation is set out, starting in New Testament times. Later in this summary history is included material on the Reformation and then the development of these rites in the Church of England in the twentieth century.

Let us begin with the Reformation, when the rite of confirmation underwent some of its most radical changes. The conservative 1549 Book of Common Prayer not only retained a rite of confirmation but re-affirmed the English mediaeval rule that 'there shall none be admitted to the Holy Communion, until such time as he be confirmed'. The 1552 revisions were more radical and the rubrics suggest that the term 'confirm' was now being used, at least partially, in a different sense. Instead of the bishop confirming the candidate by the laying on of hands, invoking the Holy Spirit, it offers a stronger sense of the candidate confirming his/her faith in the promises made by godparents at the time of baptism. The shift in the prayers is telling. The 1549 prayer runs thus:

> send down from heaven we beseech thee, (O Lord) upon them thy holy ghost . . .

In the 1552 rite we read:

> strengthen them we beseech thee, (O Lord) with thy holy ghost . . .

229 Presumably the separation of the baptism from the main Eucharist derived from an unease in the congregation to have large numbers of baptisms roughly in their main weekly worship; some would also argue that such a public setting is also difficult for families who are not regularly part of the church family.

There is still, as we can see, an invocation of the Holy Spirit to strengthen the candidate but, as we note later, the precise intention of these changes can be variously interpreted. In the rite of 1549, confirmation still appears to be a rite of chrismation with a sacramentally effective invocation of the spirit. In the rite of 1552, however, the spirit emphasizes strengthening from within.[230] These are small changes but, under the influence of Martin Bucer, they are suggestive of wider religious, societal and ideological changes. Indeed, a greater emphasis on interiority in 1552 bears witness to a world becoming less at ease with sacramentalism and increasingly concerned with personal belief. In the 1662 Book of Common Prayer, both the baptism and confirmation rites remained substantially unchanged from those accepted in the Elizabethan settlement, in the 1559 Book of Common Prayer. Confirmation remained a ratification and so, literally, a confirmation of baptismal promises. While not being 'necessary for salvation', confirmation remained integral to the rites of initiation. The rubric relating to communion was softened to read: 'And there shall none be admitted to the holy Communion, until such time as he be confirmed, or be ready and desirous to be confirmed.'

230 In the Collect the wording changes: In 1549 the third phrase runs 'send down from heaven we beseech thee, (O Lord) upon them thy Holy Ghost the comforter, with manifold gifts of grace, the spirit of wisdom and understanding . . .' In 1552 this changes to 'strengthen them, we beseech thee, (O Lord) with the Holy Ghost the comforter, and daily increase in them thy manifold gifts of grace, the spirit of wisdom and understanding . . .' There is a shift towards the cognitive from the effective through the emphasis on the gradual increasing of the gifts of the Spirit both in the Collect and in the newly interposed following prayer. The signing of the cross and the prayer that goes with it are removed in 1552. There is a clear reference in 1549 to confirming and strengthening candidates with the inward unction of the Holy Ghost. Once again the removal of this, alongside the insertion of the new material in 1552, reduces the stronger sense of sacramentality implied in 1549. This shift in emphasis is confirmed by G. Cuming in *A History of Anglican Liturgy* (London: Macmillan 1969), pp. 86–7. He notes of 1549: Confirmation is literally translated from the Sarum rite, with the one alteration that anointing is replaced by laying-on of hands, with a reference to the inward unction of the Holy Ghost; signing with the cross is kept. The service ends with the greatly shortened version of the prayer in Hermann's *Deliberatio*, one of the very few Orders to have a confirmation service at all. Cranmer is obviously copying Hermann's arrangement of the whole section, beginning with an introduction headed 'Confirmation, wherein is contained a Catechism for Children', in which Hermann's influence is clearly apparent, then printing the Catechism, and finally the actual services of confirmation. He also agrees with Hermann in giving up the use of oil and introducing the laying-on of hands. Cuming goes on to say of the 1552 rite, 'in confirmation, however, the signing with the Cross and its prayer are removed; and God is asked not to send down the Holy Spirit upon the candidates, but merely to strengthen them with him. The laying-on of hands is accompanied by a new prayer based on Hermann' (p. 113).

The proposed revision of 1927/8 effectively intended to strengthen the integrity of the rites of initiation including confirmation. The *Companion* notes: 'Confirmation underwent a more substantial theological shift, the preface claimed that, following the example of the Apostles in Acts 8, "a special gift of the Holy Spirit is bestowed through the laying on of hands with prayer".'[231] This shift re-asserts the emphasis stressed in the pneumatology of the 1549 prayer book. The renewal of baptismal vows was extended and included a renunciation, an affirmation of faith and a promise of lifelong obedience. It was the period after this that saw the publication both of a series of reports and the beginning of an intense debate on the relationship between baptism and confirmation. Leading the battle groups on behalf of confirmation was Gregory Dix who saw confirmation (as implied in 1928) as the completion of initiation by the conferring of the gift of the Spirit. Geoffrey Lampe led the opposing brigades arguing that the fullness of Christian initiation was there in baptism alone. The 1971 Ely Report chaired by Edward Roberts, the then Bishop of Ely, with Geoffrey Lampe as a key member, continued the pressure to see baptism as complete sacramental initiation. The 1980 Alternative Service Book attempted to address this controversy by opting for a complete Christian initiation being expressed in a unitary rite of baptism, confirmation and Eucharist.[232] If anything, the theology of confirmation became thinner still, although the need for confirmation as a rite for adults returning to faith, or discovering a new and active faith became more significant. The need for some form of post-baptismal rite thus increased, although its theological foundations were not secured.

Paul Avis, in a number of different essays, has taken up the argument as it has been rehearsed more recently.[233] In these articles, Avis has indicated why the notion of baptism being complete sacramental initiation has gained such wide credence. The reasons he notes are the crucial significance of baptism, the need to regain a unified rite, and the essential role baptism plays in the scheme

231 Paul Bradshaw (ed.), *A Companion to Common Worship* (London: SPCK, 2001), p. 158. (This commentary is what it says it is and has the authority as of those who produced it; it is not the 'official teaching' of the Church of England.)

232 This followed a tradition established in the 1948 and 1958 Lambeth Conferences and by the 1948 report *The Theology of Christian Initiation* and the 1958 Church of England Liturgical Commission Report *Baptism and Confirmation*.

233 See 'Christian Initiation as a Whole Process (Is Baptism "complete sacramental initiation"?)', FOAG Paper, CCU/FO/05/33. [A revised version of a paper offered to the Fifth Meissen Theological Conference]; and more recently 'Is baptism "complete sacramental initiation"?' *Theology* (London: SPCK), Vol. CXI, No. 861, May/June 2008, pp. 163–9.

of salvation. Avis argues, however, that this approach to initiation has clear fault-lines. First of all, even if we are unhappy with describing initiation as a *process*, nevertheless it is still appropriate to see initiation as an 'unfolding event', a play set in a series of acts. Secondly, within our sacramental understanding of baptism, there is the need for human response. Just as the Christian gospel implies the priority of grace, to which we as human persons respond, so baptism is one of the effective identifiers of this. Human response itself unfolds over a period of time. We wrote earlier of the journey/pilgrimage elements within Christian experience. Finally, Avis makes it clear how, in ecumenical dialogue, most notably with Baptist churches, this broader view of initiation offers its own richness. Both infant baptism as practised by some churches and adult baptism, as required in the Baptist tradition, can be seen as part of an extended process which varies within traditions.

Avis notes at one point: 'However, it is significant that *Common Worship* has not embraced BACSI [baptism as 'complete sacramental initiation']. In this respect, it continues the tradition of the Book of Common Prayer.'[234] This effectively adverts to a continuing debate for, by contrast, the *Companion to Common Worship* notes: 'The change of emphasis which now sees baptism as complete initiation has led to baptism with confirmation being a second section of the initiation services.'[235] The point is made that chrism may now be used in the baptism rite and that this effectively undermines arguments which see confirmation as the completion of the initiation rite.[236] Later we read:

> Behind all this lies a lack of clear theology of the place of confirmation. The Church of England seems to hold on to it as a necessity, but with little theological justification. One hundred and fifty years of debate have still not led to a conclusion, and the debate seems set to continue. How long will it be before the Church of England is bold enough to include confirmation as a 'pastoral rite', as did the Episcopal Church of the USA in 1979? [237]

There is certainly truth in the claim that there has been a lack of clarity about how the Church of England has viewed confirmation. This does not, however, imply that the conclusion arrived at in the *Companion* is itself a necessary one.

234 Avis, 'Is baptism "complete sacramental initiation"?', *op. cit.*, p. 163.

235 Bradshaw, *Companion, op. cit.*, p. 174.

236 Some would argue the chrism is not given full theological significance in the Common Worship rite, since it remains optional.

237 Bradshaw, *Companion, op. cit.*, p. 178.

Indeed it is not argued out theologically there. Avis too discerns a degree of theological uncertainty which calls for further debate. He notes:

> Obviously, this discussion leaves several questions unanswered. It does not clarify what the nature of the blessing or gift of the Holy Spirit imparted at confirmation is.[238]

Having asserted that baptism is not complete sacramental initiation, and that confession of one's own faith, a laying on of hands at confirmation as a sacramental action, and first communion are part of one unfolding event Avis argues that now 'we may be in a more favourable position to begin to fill out the theological and pastoral reconstruction of Christian initiation'.[239]

3. Confirmation in context

This discussion, then, moves us further in the direction of reflection upon the theology of confirmation. At this point it may help to take stock. Where precisely does the argument lie in relation to confirmation as part of an unfolding event? There is little doubt about the uncertainties which exist. So, in the Eastern tradition, initiation has continued as one unified rite which takes place generally in infancy; chrismation has not been separated out into a distinct rite of confirmation. In the West, confirmation has continued in the Roman Catholic tradition as a separate sacramental rite, but the link with the bishop has been partially severed; presbyteral confirmation is now an acceptable norm, using oil that has been episcopally consecrated. The widely acclaimed 'Lima document', *Baptism, Eucharist and Ministry* (*BEM*) does make brief explicit referent to confirmation. It notes:

> Christians differ in their understanding as to where the sign of the gift of the Spirit is to be focused. Different actions have become associated with the gifts of the Spirit. For some it is the water rite itself. For others, it is the anointing with chrism and/or the imposition of hands, which many churches call confirmation. For still others it is all three, as they see the Spirit operative throughout the rite. All agree that Christian baptism is in water and the Holy Spirit.[240]

In the Lima/*BEM* commentary, there is a sharp note on this particular paragraph:

238 *Ibid.*, p. 168.
239 *Ibid.*, p. 169.
240 *Baptism, Eucharist and Ministry* (Geneva: World Council of Churches, 1982), Faith and Order Paper. No. 111, p. 6, paragraph IV B.14.

> If baptism, as incorporation into the body of Christ, points by its very
> nature to the eucharistic sharing of Christ's body and blood, the
> question arises as to how a further and separate rite can be interposed
> between baptism and admission to communion. Those churches which
> baptize children but refuse them a share in the eucharist before such a
> rite may wish to ponder whether they have fully appreciated and
> accepted the consequences of baptism.[241]

This diverts us, of course, along another path, that of communion before
confirmation. It does, however, assume that confirmation itself is the 'gateway'
to communion. In the seventeenth century there was already a softening of
this in the rubrics of the 1662 Book of Common Prayer that allow for those
who are ready and desirous to be confirmed to be admitted to communion. In
the Church of England there is now a widespread practice among the dioceses
of admission to communion before confirmation. Such admission to
communion need not undervalue nor undermine the theological foundations
of confirmation, but rather open up the understanding of initiation as a
process or an unfolding event. The *BEM* commentary itself hints at the lifelong
nature of initiation:

> Baptism needs to be constantly reaffirmed. The most obvious forms of
> such reaffirmation is the celebration of the eucharist. The renewal of
> baptismal vows may also take place during such occasions as the annual
> celebration of the paschal mystery or during the baptism of others.[242]

This reinforces again the need to place baptism in context as part of a more
subtle and sophisticated understanding of the experience of initiation in the
Christian life.

This approach has been rehearsed frequently within the Church of England
over the past two decades. Both the report *On the Way* and the General Synod
report on the same document helped set the context here.[243] These argued in
part for a renewed commitment to a catechumenate, an approach already
embraced since the Second Vatican Council by the Roman Catholic Church in
its Rites for the Initiation of Adults (RCIA) process. Such a process both assumes
that initiation is an unfolding event and also recaptures some of the keynotes
of initiation from the early Church rooted in so-called mystagogical catechesis.

---

241 *Ibid.*, p. 5. (*Commentary*. 14. (b).)
242 *Ibid.*, p. 5. (*Commentary*. 14. (c).)
243 *On the Way: Towards an Integrated Approach to Christian Initiation* (London: Church
House Publishing, 1995). Cf. also Bradshaw, *Companion op. cit.*, p. 161.

Common Worship embraced much of this and the *Companion* notes that 'the new provision . . . places baptism as the theological centrepiece around which the rites of confirmation, affirmation of baptismal faith and reception into communion of the Church of England are clustered.'[244]

Common Worship, then, abandoned the single rite of the Alternative Service Book and opted instead for a *progression* of rites which also attempted to reclaim some of the key catechetical insights of the early Christian centuries. These reflections may assist us in gathering together what is often seen as rather disparate material as we seek to understand the theological patterns which can reasonably be seen to underpin confirmation.

At the centre of the debate over confirmation lie issues of sacramentality and the public affirmation of faith. Is confirmation a rite within which there is a clear sense of God imparting grace, or is it instead an occasion when an individual or a group of individuals publicly confess their faith and commitment to Jesus Christ as Lord? This very sharp way of putting the question itself leads to an inappropriate separation of these two essential elements. To begin with, it assumes that confirmation cannot be both/and. The *Companion's* commentary on the shift between 1549 and 1552, as we have noted, makes precisely this distinction. Indeed, it is clear that this distinction was intended in the more radical revisions of 1552. Although reference to the action of the Holy Spirit is not lost, it is possible to argue that the revisions of 1552 do pull the rite in a direction based more upon cognitive assent than upon sacramental efficacy. There is no dispute over the fact of these changes and the intention of some sort of shift of emphasis. There remains debate over whether there is a deliberate intention to move from an effective to a cognitive understanding between 1549 and 1552. Revisionist views of the history of the Reformation tend to reinforce the notion that a more Protestant and less overtly sacramental interpretation was intended.[245]

In a multitude of different ways the Reformers throughout Europe were keen to move from an apparent tradition of superstition to a tradition where the word was proclaimed and where individuals thereby embraced the faith in words and not simply through an *effective* sacramental faith. Individual confession of faith affected all aspects of the Church's life from worship to an appreciation of vocation or calling by God. This affected not only the Reformed churches but

---

244 Bradshaw, *Companion, op. cit.,* p. 161.

245 For general background see D. MacCulloch, *Tudor Church Militant* (London: Allen Lane, 2000); and D. MacCulloch, *Thomas Cranmer* (New Haven: Yale University Press, 1997).

also Roman Catholicism through the Council of Trent. There too the direct voice of God to the individual would mark out vocation.

The rediscovery of initiation as an unfolding event, or as a pathway with key milestones, can bring together both these sets of insights, the sacramental and the verbal. In the early Church the pattern of setting out during Lent on a process of spiritual training took the candidates and the church community forward toward passiontide, Holy Week and Easter in a manner which embraced both the didactic and the sacramental, the intellectual and the doxological. Some indeed have argued that such a combined process reaches back into the Gospels and may indeed explain the shaping of the passion by the four evangelists. Did the passion narratives originate from teaching, worship and an embryonic sacramental life lived out in the holy sites within Jerusalem? Putting aside such conjecture, we do know that such a tradition had developed by the fourth century with the pilgrimage patterns associated with Egeria.

Confirmation, then, should be understood as part of this larger unfolding pattern of initiation; that is, not as a crude 'gateway' to communion, but instead as a sacramental and confessional milestone along the journey. Such an understanding has a number of merits. Across civilizations there has been a common tradition of some sort of maturity 'rite of passage' which allows both the individual and the community to embrace this stage of development. It is there in the Jewish tradition of the *bar mitzvah*; it even developed in the atheistic culture of the former Soviet Union and its satellites.[246] This should not be seen as a means of validating the practice of confirmation, but rather as acknowledging this element within the rite. This relates directly to the affirmation or confession of faith which also relates to the tradition of catechesis both in the early Church and as rediscovered since the Second Vatican Council. Such a process relates also to a sacramental understanding of the nature of confirmation within the broader pattern of an unfolding pattern of initiation. Confession of faith and an understanding of God's gracious action are not juxtaposed, but are part of one and the same event. God's gracious act and our response lie at the heart of the baptismal covenant. Indeed God's gracious act is frequently seen by Anglicans as one of the crucial reasons for the practice of infant baptism too. The laying on of hands and chrism stand alongside the decision and the affirmation of faith and are not set in contradistinction to each other. They

---

246 J. Thrower, *Marxism-Leninism as the Civil Religion of Soviet Society* (Lampeter: Edwin Mellen Press, 1992), Studies in Religion and Society, Vol. 30.

also speak eloquently for some candidates about an appropriate rite of passage.

In its introduction to baptism and the initiation rites, the Liturgical Commission's commentary begins plainly with the affirmation: 'Baptism is the sacramental beginning of the Christian life.'[247] In itself this is a modest, but significant claim. Just a few lines further on it is stated more eloquently and within a clearer theological context: 'Those who are exploring the way of Christ for the first time set their feet on a path that leads to salvation.'[248]

This is not to underplay the essential nature of baptism, but rather to imply that the journey in God begins here and effectively lasts a lifetime. It is also sacramental and as such is an event, an action and a liturgy which does not solely relate to an individual, but to the individual's place within the wider community, within the Body of Christ. What does this say, if anything, about the theological significance of the various unfolding moments on the path to which baptism is the gateway and a clue to all that follows? The beginnings of an answer may lie in the prayer which was first introduced in the 1552 revision of the Book of Common Prayer and which remained there in 1559 and 1662. It is the prayer used at the laying on of hands:

> Defend, O Lord, this thy Child [*or* this thy Servant] with thy heavenly grace, that he may continue there for ever; and daily increase in thy Holy Spirit more and more, until he come into thy everlasting kingdom.[249]

There are two key elements in this prayer, which remains mandatory and is to be said by all after the laying on of hands in the *Common Worship* order for confirmation. First of all, in a manner worthy of the Reformers, the prayer begins with a direct reference to God's grace: 'Defend, O Lord, this thy Servant with thy heavenly grace . . .' Whatever the uncertainties may be about the sacramental nature of the rite, the bishop calls for God's grace to defend the person confirmed. In the *Common Worship* version it is in the plural. Then secondly we hear: 'daily increase in your Holy Spirit more and more, until they come to your everlasting kingdom'.

An emphasis on the continuing growth of the person (and so the Church) in grace is directly stated. This is further reinforced by the prayer interposed after

247 *Common Worship: Christian Initiation, op. cit.,* p. 325.
248 *Ibid.,* p. 325.
249 *The Book of Common Prayer* (Oxford: Oxford University Press, 1662) 'Order of Confirmation'.

this in 1552. Here then, in this Reformation rite, we encounter the notion of being 'on the way', of this being part of a lifetime's journey continuing 'until they come to your everlasting kingdom'. Even the shift in the collect, from 1549 to 1552, to using the word 'strengthen' suggests this sense of continuing growth in the spirit. Might this offer us a clue to a theological understanding of confirmation and all that follows along the continuing journey?

4. Continuing theology

Where have we got to so far then? What are the key elements which we cannot ignore? First is a concern that Christian initiation should itself be missionary in its implications. So, for example, we should ask, Do our church buildings challenge people to understand the nature of the gospel simply by how they are ordered? Do font and altar point to entry and continuing nourishment? Then we are challenged to see how the rites themselves look outward to the community if they are to be embracingly missionary. This in itself requires initiation to be part of an unfolding event, as indeed is human life itself. This leads us to place the different elements of initiation within a broader theological context which bursts the walls and boundaries which have unhelpfully constrained our understanding of baptism, confirmation, admission to communion and indeed the Eucharist itself. The 1662 prayer with the laying on of hands at confirmation suggests a pattern of continuous growth in God throughout our lives. What might this mean about the imparting of grace or the reception of God as Holy Spirit through the initiation process and within the Eucharist? This also has further implications for our understanding of ordination.

It is easy to assume that the understanding and use of confirmation and baptism have remained static. This is far from the truth, of course. The *Publick Baptism as Such as Are of Riper Years* entered the Book of Common Prayer only in 1662. The rite was deemed necessary following the years of the Commonwealth when infants had not been baptized. At times, confirmation was non-existent for Anglicans, when bishops were not resident or when Anglicans lived in colonies overseas. The pattern that is now often seen as the 'norm' – bishops travelling round the diocese to confirm in parishes – is a Victorian development that was aided by the growth of the railways and turnpike roads and the expansion in numbers of suffragan bishops. So, first of all then, patterns of initiation have changed. In recent years there has once again been a growth in the number of confirmations happening in cathedrals, with larger numbers. This has largely been driven by theological concerns.

Such confirmations emphasize the corporate element of the initiation rites; there is a clear sense of the Church at such occasions. Secondly, with imaginative use of cathedral buildings there can be an effective use of a staged rite. The rite of baptism occurs at the font, hopefully near to the church door. The entire congregation then move on to the place of confirmation, perhaps at the crossing, if the cathedral is so designed. Finally, communion happens at the high altar, probably with the congregation standing as one body. The giving of the candle and 'sending out' gives an opportunity for one more stage in the unfolding process of initiation. There is a third strand to such confirmations inasmuch as the bishop confirms in his church and may take the opportunity to spend a longer time with the candidates in catechesis, rehearsal, in some sort of social gathering and finally in the baptism-confirmation-eucharistic rite itself.

Such an approach to the liturgy is also informed by the anthropological term *liminality*. This refers to liminal experiences, threshold experiences, which relate either to 'stages' in our life or to becoming part of a new community or group. Baptism and confirmation (and even the sending) are *liminal* moments in the life of the Christian believer. This is true, even with those who are baptized and/or confirmed but who remain on the margins of the Church.

What precisely, however, do we believe is going on theologically in the confirmation rite itself? Returning to an earlier point, we noted that baptism is the clue to all that follows. In any catechesis, this is the obvious place to begin. Byzantine fonts were designed to look like 'walk-in' stone coffins near to the entrance of the church; the symbolism of dying and rising with Christ is clearly made. Other images can be explored too: liberation and salvation as with the Israelites being brought out of the water at the Red Sea; or cleansing as a sign of repentance and then turning again as is made clear in the decision. These images also reinforce the experience of liminality. The waters of baptism are a powerful sacramental image and at the same time a proven catechetical impulse from which to begin. Bound up in the sacrament of initiation, however, are a number of different elements. Thomas Seville has helpfully set these out in an essay on confirmation. Seville makes it clear that baptism by water, from the earliest centuries, appears to have been accompanied by other signs, including the laying on of hands and the administering of oil in anointing.[250] There is a fairly clear consensus among many recent scholars that rebirth in the Spirit through the waters is operative in terms of a theology of

---

250 T. Seville CR, 'Confirmation', unpublished paper for the Faith and Order Advisory Group.

salvation. One of the difficulties in the fragmentation of the rite of Christian initiation is that the different signs also become separated. This in itself easily leads to somewhat crude questions being asked about precisely what is happening alongside each of these sacramental signs – laying on of hands, anointing, dipping (or immersing and dipping) three times in water. Thus Seville points to similar difficulties in understanding the meaning of chrismation in confirmation.[251]

Seville's detailed analysis indicates how difficult it is to separate out different elements of the sacramental into separate 'theological moments' within the different rites. All these different actions with water, oil and laying on of hands are better seen as part of one organic whole. If that is the case, then the mistake is to attempt to focus God's action in the Holy Spirit at any specific moment within any of the rites. All of the signs are significant and important but they are not to be analysed in such a way as to suggest that God acts at one moment only. The *Companion to Common Worship* makes a helpful comparison here:

> Much debate on ancient liturgical texts asks questions that our forbears in faith would not have asked and makes distinctions they would not consider. Just as today an Orthodox would not understand why you would ask whether the Spirit was conferred at water baptism or chrismation, so too the ancient writers of liturgical texts would not understand the question. It comes out of a Western interest in the 'moment' of consecration. Rather they would affirm that the whole rite is both pneumatic and baptismal and the one cannot be divided from the other.[252]

The Western tradition has thus been much more concerned with instrumental questions which have tried to identify key sacramental actions with specific theological actions of God. If this mistake is avoided it opens up questions about the nature of baptism, confirmation and the Eucharist in a far more fruitful and rich way. We can affirm that God's grace is active in the Eucharist, not simply immediately after the institution narrative, but throughout the celebration of the entire rite. So, too, we need to see baptism, confirmation and the Eucharist holistically; the grace of God is made available in initiation throughout the unfolding event even when that event unfolds in a series of episodes which are sometimes chronologically fairly distinct from each other.

251 *Ibid.*, pp. 11, 13–14.
252 Bradshaw, *Companion, op. cit.*, pp. 175–6.

Perhaps, at this point, however, it is worth noting one danger of seeing Christian initiation as an unfolding process. Such an understanding of initiation risks dissolving the initiation into the theme of discipleship or into a more general understanding of the life of faith. While initiation into the mystery of the divine life is a life-long process, nonetheless there is a focus upon the sacramental events that *begin* that process. That is, on the one hand there is a life of ongoing initiation and, on the other, events of initiation. In the same way that it is now proper to say that the whole eucharistic prayer is consecratory – and not one particular, positivistically understood, moment or set of words within that service – nevertheless it is *this* prayer at *this* time which is consecratory. As space- and time-bound creatures we do not have an unmediated access to what is universal and eternal. We understand such verities in and through events in time. In a world understood through the lens of the incarnation it is the particular which mediates the universal. So it is that sacramental and efficacious *events* mediate to us the significance and meaning of what may be a process that takes more time, even a life-time. The gift of grace, of course, can neither be commanded nor captured by any set of words but it is always understood not as something general but as something particular and personal. It is important that this understanding of the rites of initiation, as efficacious *events* that signify for us that which takes place over longer periods of our lives, is not lost.

So this understanding of Christian initiation – as an unfolding event signified by these particular events – opens up on a broader front theological considerations which again have been too easily constrained by an emphasis on a 'moment of the Spirit', or indeed, different *moments* of the Spirit, whilst also sometimes seeking qualitative differences in what the Spirit effects or transforms in these moments. Seville helpfully notes: 'In entering into the reality of Jesus Christ and His Church, the neophyte enters into a relation of participation with Jesus Christ and the Spirit, a share in the relation of the Son of the Father.' [253]

This is an essential passage since it moves us from a rather 'fundamentalist' form of pneumatology in Christian initiation to a full Trinitarian understanding automatically implied by the threefold dipping and the threefold questioning at the decision. But even at this point there are real dangers. In the Alternative Service Book, the threefold decision opted for a form of 'modalism', separating out the Father as Creator, the Son as Redeemer and the Spirit as Sanctifier. In

253 Seville, *op. cit.*, p. 17.

Common Worship this is avoided by making all three questions turn around Christ as Saviour, as Lord and as the way, the truth and the life. In Pauline terms we are baptized into Christ, but this is to imply a full engagement with the life of God as Trinity.

As we try to regain a sense of Christian initiation as being a continuing initiation into and participation in the life of God, efficaciously marked by sacramental events, we may be helped by recovering the use of a term more often encountered in the Eastern tradition, that of perichoresis. The 'Cyprus Statement', *The Church of the Triune God*, of the International Commission for Anglican–Orthodox Theological Dialogue argues that the life of God is dynamic. That is, God as eternally hospitable seeks to draw the believer into his life. So, the terms Father, Son and Holy Spirit 'speak of identities that eternally constitute each other in their mutual relationships'.

> Affirming the independent reality of the Spirit [as a Person, alongside the more obviously personal terms Father and Son] implies that the perfect love of Father and Son, the completeness of giving and receiving in God, is not all that should be said about the divine life. There is no exclusivity or mutual self-absorption in the relation of Father and Son, because there exists also the relation between the Father and the Spirit, and the Son and the Spirit. Thus God's life is a dynamic, eternal and unending movement of self-giving.[254]

However, because God is transcendent and 'ever-more' than himself, this immanent life of self-giving also becomes 'the free out-flowing of the Father's self-giving: in the economy of salvation the Holy Spirit offers us a share in the divine life to created beings'.[255] God's life is offered for all and is that into which all are called to participate. It is the Spirit which takes us beyond any immanent self-contained Father-Son 'binitarianism' in the Godhead and marks that openness in the Godhead, constituted by this mutual self-giving love, which invites the creature to share in God's life.

Perichoresis, then with its understanding of mutuality and relationship within the Godhead, combined with concepts of *theosis* (or deification) gives a richer understanding of the Holy Spirit's interpenetration of the life of each individual human person. Through a spiritual process of adoption and filiation, the

---

254 *The Church of the Triune God: The Cyprus Statement agreed by the International Commission for Anglican–Orthodox Theological Dialogue* (London: The Anglican Communion Office, 2006), p. 26, II, 5.

255 *Ibid.*, p. 26, II, 5.

believer is caught up into the relationship which Christ shares with the Father (Rom. 8.15, 23; Gal. 4.6).[256] The Spirit forms the believer into the likeness of Christ (*theosis*). Indeed, just as the baptism of Jesus does not represent a moment of conversion but an 'affirmation, through the Spirit, of Jesus' relation to the Father', which is his divine Sonship, so too the descent of the Spirit at baptism today marks the on-going process of filiation and deification in the life of the believer. As the Cyprus Statement puts it:

> [Jesus'] baptism is an initiation into the whole of his mission culminating in the cross [and so] baptism unites us with Christ in his death and resurrection (Rom. 6.1–11). At our baptism the Spirit forms Christ in us, and enables us to share in Christ's crucifixion and resurrection. Then we begin to live in the Spirit . . . because the liberation of our humanity for the life among God's people, accomplished in Jesus' death and resurrection, becomes a reality in us.[257]

These concepts of perichoresis, deification and filiation may help us appreciate better the relationship between the intellectual, spiritual and liturgical in relation to Christian initiation as the believer is caught up into the life of God within the Church. Such an understanding also helps avoid the fragmentation of theological discourse to which the Western tradition has been prone and which the Caroline Divines of the seventeenth century did much to repair.[258] The Caroline tradition rediscovered the integral nature of theology bringing doctrinal, moral and ascetic reflection together as one. Entering into Christ through the whole process of initiation implies a turning from sin, an entering into a living relationship with God in worship – a relationship which the processions of the divine Trinity exhibits – and a reshaping of our lives in God. The Caroline Divines similarly saw ascetic, doctrinal and moral theology all of a piece.

The Western tradition has by no means been entirely devoid of this continuous perichoretic theological understanding. We were reminded of it two generations ago by Charles Williams, especially in his book *The Descent of the Dove*, but indeed more widely, in his re-capturing of the use of the term *co-*

---

256 *Ibid.*, p. 26, II, 6.

257 *Ibid.*, p. 36, II, 40.

258 H. McAdoo makes this point in his analysis of the Caroline tradition in *The Structure of Caroline Moral Theology* (London: Longmans Green, 1949). See especially Chapter VI. Here McAdoo argues for the unity of moral and ascetic theology and for this as an integrating structure for all theological disclosure.

inherence.[259] Williams develops the term coinherence, which in the tradition is often used synonymously with perichoresis, in a number of sophisticated and interrelated patterns. So in an incarnational and participatory mode it draws together spirit and matter. Thus he notes of the Alexandrian school of Christology in the early Church: 'Yet there is about them a sense of the *naturalness* [his italics] of Christianity, as distinguished from its catastrophic supernaturalness.'[260]

In his postscript to *The Descent of the Dove*, Williams develops this further in relation to the Church and its place in the world. This relationship of Church to world is made especially clear in the rites of initiation. At baptism, godparents stand for the candidate in his/her worldliness and naturalness. It is brought together in confirmation: 'It is this co-inherence which, at the confirmation, he (the candidate) confesses and ratifies.' [261]

For Williams, however, such ratification is not a purely intellectual assent. Instead it implies too the fullness of the indwelling Spirit of God by means of which all coinheres. This coinherence or perichoresis, then, proceeds from God in Trinity and binds together spirit and matter, human and divine. The sacramental rites in their totality mirror and make effective such coinherence in the life of the individual believer and of the Church of God as it lives for the world.

Rather more recently, Gavin Ashenden, bringing this together in his new study of Charles Williams, writes:

> The habitual tendency in Christian theology to separate spirit and matter has diverted religious and visionary energy from the practicalities of much of everyday life. The secular has been stripped of

259 C. Williams, *The Descent of the Dove: A Short History of the Holy Spirit in the Church* (London: Longmans, 1939). See also particularly his essay 'The Way of Exchange', in *'The Image of The City' and Other Essays* (Oxford: Oxford University Press, 1958).

260 Williams, *Descent, op.cit.*, p. 37. See also P. L. Gavrilyuk, 'The Retrieval of Deification: How a Once Despised Archaism Became an Ecumenical Desideratum', *Modern Theology* 25.4, Oct. 2009, pp. 647–59. Gavrilyuk's discussion of a recent interest in deification perhaps shows that Charles Williams' own work on this (from an earlier generation) is now reflected in a broader ecumenical trend for which themes of *theosis*, coinherence and perichoresis are important. This is part of a wider retrieval of Christian Platonism, which tradition is already well represented in Anglicanism, for example, in the persons of the Cambridge Platonists such as Ralph Cudworth. Some would also argue that the influence on Anglicanism can be traced back to the conciliarists and notably to the thought of Nicholas of Cusa.

261 Williams, *Descent, op. cit.*, pp. 234–5.

the sacred and the energy for renewal and transformation that the sacred carried with it . . . Williams's philosophical and theological healing of the division yields two consequences. Each of them has the capacity for transformation. [262]

The two consequences include 'a theological vision for the integration of matter and spirit'.[263]

Later he notes: 'Williams's vision of co-inherence provides the justification for linking the progress of the human condition perceived in classical theological terms with the need for social and political transformation.'[264]

Christian initiation and the journey which it implies is just such a transformation. Seen as an unfolding series of episodes, with the grace of God continuing but still focused in sacramental acts, baptism, confirmation, the affirmation of faith and a eucharistically centred life offer a realistic opportunity for transformation. Ultimately this takes us full circle to those two separated communities on the north western edge of that Yorkshire town and within that ancient university. Our vision of Christian initiation needs to be able to bring them together. It is God co-inherent in humanity and nothing less that is offered.[265]

---

262 G. Ashenden, *Alchemy and Integration* (Kent, Ohio: Kent State University Press, 2008), p. 233.

263 *Ibid.*, p. 233.

264 *Ibid.*, p. 234.

265 I am grateful to the Revd Dr Paul Avis and Dr Martin Davie for helpful comments on the text, and to the Revd Dr Matthew Bullimore for some help in the initial research for the paper and later comments.